# STARTING A BUSINESS

## A 7-STEP SYSTEM TO SUCCESSFULLY LAUNCH YOUR OWN BUSINESS IN 30 DAYS

### WALTER GRANT

# CONTENTS

# INTRODUCTION

---

"There's no shortage of remarkable ideas, what's missing is the will to execute them."

— SETH GODIN

---

A lot of people dream of quitting their jobs and starting their own businesses, but, for many, this only remains a dream as they continue suffering in a job they hate. There are many reasons why these people are unable to turn their dreams into reality. For some, the greatest problem is a lack of ideas. For others, it's an inability to turn their ideas into successful businesses. Others are afraid that their idea might end up failing, and they have no idea how to validate their ideas before investing their time and money into their new business.

You have probably asked yourself one of these questions:

- Can I launch a business without prior experience of running one?
- Can I have my own business running within 30 days?
- How do I even come up with a business idea? Do I really need a business plan, and how do I create one?
- How do I even promote my business to potential customers?
- How do I protect my ideas from being stolen or copied while I look for investors or partners?

If you have asked yourself any of these questions, you already know how difficult it can be to start your own business, especially when it is your first time. What if you had someone to hold your hand and guide you through the entire process of starting a business from scratch and growing it into a successful business?

That is what this book is about. In each chapter, I share all I have accumulated in decades of starting new businesses, joining start-ups, and being successful at most of them. In this book, you will find easy-to-follow actionable steps to go from having no idea of where to start to have a fully operational business within 30 days.

Some of the things you are going to learn in this book include:

- The mindset you need to adopt in order to increase your chances of success.
- How to come up with great business ideas and validate them.
- How to write a business plan.
- How to secure funding and manage your finances.
- How to sell yourself and your business to customers.
- How to hire the perfect team.
- How to legalize your business and protect your ideas.

- How to launch and grow your business.
- What's more, you will receive a schedule of everything you need to do for each of these 30 days to ensure that your business is up and running by the 30$^{th}$ day.

# THE ENTREPRENEURIAL MINDSET AND BRAINSTORMING IDEAS

I t is a great thing that you are thinking of starting your own business and taking charge of your life. However, before you take the plunge, you need to know to note that starting and running a business is not for everyone. According to a report by the Global Entrepreneurship Monitor (GEM), close to 14% of the US adult population (over 25 million Americans) are starting or running new businesses. Unfortunately, data from the Bureau of Labor Statistics show that more than half of all new businesses fail within before their fifth birthday.

Why this huge rate of failure? While there are many reasons why a new business might fail, it mostly boils down to the mindset of the business owner. If you want your business venture to be successful, you need to learn how to think like an entrepreneur. Without an entrepreneurial mindset, your business might not even live to see its first birthday.

If you observe the world's most successful entrepreneurs, you will notice that they all have a similar mindset in their approach to challenges, attitudes towards risks and mistakes, learning, and decision making.

Successful entrepreneurs do not sit and wait for things to happen. Instead, they are always taking action, creating their own opportunities, and looking for ways to remain relevant. Whereas others see challenges as setbacks, entrepreneurs see them as opportunities. They are constantly trying to learn and improve themselves. They are attentive to their environment and are quick to identify and take advantage of business opportunities.

This mindset and approach to life is what sets apart successful entrepreneurs from everyone else. It is what keeps them moving forward even in situations where giving up seems to be the logical thing to do. If you do not want your business venture to be part of the half that goes belly up before its fifth year, you must learn to think like an entrepreneur before you embark on the entrepreneurial journey.

Some people are born with an entrepreneurial mindset. Being an entrepreneur comes easily to them. Fortunately, it is a trait that can be learned, assimilated, imbibed, and put to practice by those not born with it. You can teach yourself to think like a successful entrepreneur by following any of the tips down below.

**Find Your Passion**

All successful entrepreneurs are extremely passionate about what they do. Their business consumes their whole lives, and they are willing to make big sacrifices. For instance, Facebook founder Mark Zuckerberg decided to drop out of Harvard to bring his idea of a social network to life. Similarly, Jeff Bezos quit a very lucrative job on Wall Street to start Amazon. The passion for what they are doing is what keeps entrepreneurs going, even when things do not seem to be going their way.

To become a successful entrepreneur, you need to learn how to follow your passion. Don't get into business just because you want to make money, or because the life of an entrepreneur looks glamorous. It is not. There will be lots of difficulties and challenges, and thoughts of quitting. In these moments, it is your passion that will keep you going.

## Get Comfortable With Risk

Being an entrepreneur is synonymous with risk. Starting a business is a risky affair, you never know whether it will work or not until you do it. For instance, after making millions from the sale of PayPal, tech billionaire Elon Musk put all his money into his passion project, SpaceX. He was left with no money, yet SpaceX was blowing through money without making any. At some point, he was so broke that he had to survive on loans from his friends. But he kept at it. soon, he was back on his feet quickly after signing a multibillion dollar deal with NASA, which also saved his company from collapse.

Would you be willing to take such a huge risk? Successful entrepreneurs are not afraid of taking risks. They have a high tolerance for risk. Similarly, if you want to be a successful entrepreneur, you have to constantly step out of your comfort zone. However, this does not mean that you should take risks blindly. Instead, you should weigh the risk, assess its potential benefits, and put in place measures to minimize the risk. Most importantly, do not be afraid of failing. Failure is merely another opportunity to learn and improve.

## Adopt A Goal-Oriented Attitude

Successful entrepreneurs know that they are responsible for the outcomes of their lives and their businesses. They know that success is not a matter of chance – it is their sole responsibility. Therefore, they don't live life aimlessly. They set goals for themselves, whether in life or in business and make sure every action they take is geared towards achieving those goals.

To be a successful entrepreneur, you need to adopt the same mindset. Have goals for every sphere of your life. Before you start your business, determine what goals you want to achieve, when, and the steps you need to take to get there. This will provide you with direction and will ensure you don't waste your time and energy on things that are not beneficial to you or your business.

**Learn To View Challenges As Opportunities**

Most people try as much as possible to avoid challenges. When they encounter a difficulty, they either give up or change course. Successful entrepreneurs, on the other hand, understand that challenges are a part of life. When they encounter challenges, they don't back down or give up. Instead, they look for ways to overcome the challenges, and in so doing, discover opportunities most people would miss.

As an entrepreneur, you have to be ready for and comfortable with facing challenges and problems. Starting and running your business is not going to be easy. You will encounter endless obstacles and setbacks. Your attitude towards these obstacles is what will determine whether you will be successful or not.

## Learn To Think Strategically

To start and run a successful business, you need to become a master strategist. You need to be able to spot opportunities and quickly determine the best way to take advantage of them. You need to learn how to attract prospects, turn them into paying clients and keep them coming back. You need to be able to set your business apart from the competition, give it an edge, and remain relevant. All these require constant planning, reviewing your results, and optimizing your strategy.

## Understand The Ecosystem

Businesses do not operate in a vacuum. They are surrounded by other businesses, customers, and governmental regulations, all of which have an impact on your business. To be a successful entrepreneur, you need to understand not only your business, but also the ecosystem in which it operates, or else you might be caught flat-footed by unanticipated change. For instance, what if the government passes a new policy that has a direct effect on the future of your business.

Do you take the time to consider what such policies mean for your business? As an entrepreneur, you must observe the entire ecosystem in which you operate and watch out for any changes that might have an impact on your business.

**Be Driven By Your Vision**

Successful entrepreneurs do not act blindly nor in haste. They have a vision for themselves and their business. They know where they are going, and what they are trying to achieve. They dedicate their lives to following this vision and do away with anything that might be distracting them from it. All their resources—time, money, and effort—are expended in line with this vision. Most importantly, this vision keeps them on the straight and narrow even in the face of challenges.

If you want to become successful in business, you need to develop a vision for yourself. Why did you start your business? Where do you see yourself in five or ten years? From there, everything you do in business should take you closer to this vision. When things get tough, remembering why you started will push you to overcome the obstacles you are facing. Have a vision. Plan for it. Execute it.

## Be Disciplined

To become a successful entrepreneur, you need to be focused. You need to prioritize your business and forget everything else that does not contribute to its success. You need to put in a lot of time and effort, to work when you would rather be doing something else. Maintaining the level of effort, energy, mental stamina, and drive needed to make a success of a business requires utmost discipline. You can compare being in business to going to the gym every morning. Sometimes, the thought of leaving your comfortable bed to go work out is not appealing. Sometimes, it is too cold weather, feeling tired, etc. But if you want to meet your fitness goals, you have to remain disciplined, stick to the plan and go to the gym anyway. Similar to what is expected of an entrepreneur.

## HOW TO COME UP WITH PROFITABLE BUSINESS IDEAS

We have discussed how to instill the entrepreneurial mindset. It's now time to seriously decide which business you are going to start.

Many of those who are thinking about starting a new business find it very challenging to come up with a business idea. Not just any idea, but an idea that will be the foundation for a successful business.

The good news is that there are millions of business ideas. The problem is not a lack of ideas, but the execution of those ideas. You just need to know where and how to look, be open-minded, and creative. As time goes on, getting into the habit of consciously trying to identify business opportunities will become second nature to you, and you'll start coming up with more business ideas than you will ever need.

Let's take a look at some surprisingly simple ways of coming up with business ideas.

### Find Problems That Need Solving

This is the easiest way to come up with business ideas. Profit-making businesses exist in answer to a problem or need. Companies like Uber and Lyft exist because they make it easy and convenient for people to hail cabs. A business like Airbnb is successful because it makes it easy and convenient for people to find accommodation when traveling. Bottled water companies exist because they give thirsty people easy and convenient access to drinking water. Amazon exists because it makes it possible for people to shop from the comfort of their homes. When Henry Ford founded the Ford Motor Company, he did it because he saw a way to help people travel faster and more conveniently. Digital marketing agencies exist because other businesses need help with their digital marketing. Basically, every business exists because it solves a certain problem for some people, and if you can find problems that need solving, you have a profitable business idea on your hands.

So, how do you identify problems that need solving?

A good way to get good at identifying problems is to analyze your own problems. As you go through your daily activities, watch out for anything that gets you frustrated, or something that makes you wish you had someone to help you with. This could be anything, from mowing your lawn, walking your dog, or toilet training your cat, to writing your resume, creating Facebook ads for your business, or sending out emails to your prospects. It does not matter what the issue is, chances are that a lot of other people have that same issue and are willing to pay to have it solved..

This is how many successful businesses started. For instance, in 1984, billionaire Sir Richard Branson was trying to get to the British Virgin Islands, but he was stuck in Puerto Rico with other travelers after their flight got canceled. Instead of sitting and waiting till another flight was available (see what I said about people with the entrepreneurial mindset not waiting for things to happen), Branson found out the cost of chartering a plane, divided the cost by the number of those stranded at the Puerto Rican airport, and sold them one-way tickets to the British Virgin Islands. This is how Virgin Atlantic was born.

Similarly, during an adventurous surfing trip to Indonesia, Nick Woodman was frustrated that he couldn't find amateur photographers with equipment that would allow them to capture close-range, high-action shots of him as he surfed. He figured that there had to be other people with the same problem, and that was how the idea for the GoPro was born.

If you get in the habit of watching for things that frustrate you as you go about your day, you will soon start realizing that many of them represent business opportunities. Alternatively, you can find ideas by listening to the complaints and frustrations of your family and friends. Does your spouse complain about how they wish they had someone to take their car to the repair shop because both of you are busy at work? That is a business opportunity right there. Is your friend complaining about how they never have time to walk their dog? That is another business opportunity right there.

A business idea can be as simple as fixing an everyday problem.

**Solve Future Problems**

Aside from solving current problems, you can also come up with business ideas that are solutions to future problems. It not only gives you time to find a solution, but it also gives you a headstart and edge over your competition when the problem does rear its head.

Once again, tech billionaire Elon Musk provides a

great example of a business idea that is a solution to a future problem: Tesla. Tesla is into automobile production like a lot of other firms except they are delving into electric cars. This is ahead of the inevitable fossil fuel shortage that will render gasoline-powered cars obsolete. By the time the world realizes fossil fuels are becoming scarce, the Tesla brand will already be well-established and other car manufacturers will be playing catch-up.

You can be like Elon and look for a need that is not yet apparent and start making plans to solve it before it becomes mainstream.

**Think Of Ways To Meet Current Needs In An Ever-Evolving World**

Human needs have remained relatively the same throughout time. From physical needs like food, water, shelter, medicine, and clothing, to emotional needs like love, companionship, a sense of belonging, and socializing, what has changed is the manner these needs are met.

A hundred years ago, an ancient chief would have ordered the drummer to sound his drums to notify the people of an impending war. Today, US President Donald Trump does the same thing through

Twitter. In the days before the agrarian revolution, to get food, people had to go out to hunt or gather edible roots, fruits, and shrubs. Today, you get food by walking into a restaurant or going into the grocery store. Same needs, but different ways of solving them.

You can come up with profitable business ideas by trying to find convenient ways to solve needs in a world that are constantly evolving. For instance, the need to see and communicate with other people who are not in the same location as us is solved using video calls. Well, as the world continues evolving and as technology advances, you could have a great business opportunity by finding a better or more advanced way of solving this need, such as through hologram calls, which allow you to see the other person as if you are in the same room with them, instead of seeing them on a screen.

**Cost-effective Solutions**

Rechargeable batteries, automatic lighting, solar-powered items are all money-saving items. They give buyers an option that lets them spend less on a particular need or resource. Only a small percentage of the world is stupendously rich while the rest run on budgets and cost-saving. If you can think up an idea that will save people money in the long run, you have got yourself a winner. Your idea doesn't have to be original. Lights were invented a long time ago but automatic lights haven't been around for a very long time. In this case, the automatic lights help the consumer save money, therefore, it is more cost-effective and more likely to be purchased. The point is, people are always looking for ways to save money, and as a business owner you need to have this in mind.

### Find A Way To Make People's Lives Easier

Think of all the things you own whose sole purpose is to make your life easier. You own a microwave, not because you cannot warm your food on the stove, but because it is easier to warm it in the microwave. You can buy things from your local store, but you choose to order them online because it is easier for you. Robotic vacuum cleaners are becoming increasingly popular because they make cleaning your house easy. Just switch them on and continue watching Netflix as the robot vacuum cleaner does the job for you. Heck, even Netflix is worth billions because it makes it easy and convenient for people to find cool shows to watch.

Start thinking of simple ways you can make

everyday activities easier. Think it would be much easier to read a book without having to hold it in your hands? How about you come up with a hands-free book holder. Think it would be easier if you had somewhere to place your handbag when driving? How about you come up with a removable handbag hook that hangs your handbag behind the car seat?

Some of these things might seem trivial, but you might be surprised at the number of people who would be willing to pay for a solution that makes these things easy for them. And the best part is that you don't have to come up with something entirely new. If you can make improvements to already existing products or services and make life easier in the process, you have a business idea right there!

**Turn Your Hobby Into A Business**

This has become a very popular path to coming up with business ideas over the last decade. Do you have something you enjoy doing for fun, or do you have something that you are good at but have never really considered a professional skill? If you have any such activity or skill, try brainstorming on ways to monetize it. The good thing is that just about any hobby or skill can be turned into a business.

For instance, if you are good at playing the guitar, you can start a guitar-teaching business. If you are good at creating crafts, you can turn it into a business by making and selling your crafts. If you enjoy writing, you can turn your passion for writing into a business by starting a freelance writing agency. If you enjoy calligraphy, you can turn it into a business by creating awesome fonts and selling them online. If you enjoy spending your time on social media, start a social media marketing agency.

If you have something you enjoy doing and something you are good at, that's a business idea you are sitting on right there. All you need to do is to figure out a way to start making money from it. Since you will be starting a business around something you enjoy doing and are good at, it will be a lot easier for you. However, you should keep in mind that once you start a business around your hobby, it might become less enjoyable, because you will sometimes be required to do it even when you don't feel like it.

These are just some of the easiest ways of coming up with business ideas. There are several other paths to coming up with great business ideas. The point here is that if you know how to look and make a conscious effort to do it, you can easily have an endless supply of great business ideas.

## HOW TO VALIDATE YOUR BUSINESS IDEA AND DETERMINE IF IT WILL BE PROFITABLE AND SUCCESSFUL

So, you have read and imbibed the previous sections, come up with a great business idea, and are now all excited and ready to launch your business. Not so fast though!

Just because you have a business idea does not mean it will be successful. Many failed businesses started as great ideas in the minds of their owners, therefore, it is of high importance that you validate your idea and make sure it is a viable and profitable one. After all, you don't want to spend your time, money, and energy on an idea that is doomed to fail right from the start.

While there are various approaches to validating a business idea, knowing whether an idea is viable boils down to three things:

- Determining whether people have the problem you are trying to solve.

- Determining whether they are willing to pay money to solve the problem.
- Determining whether they are willing to pay money for the solution you are offering.

You can easily find out these three things by asking yourself the following questions:

## Is There Any Competition In The Space I Am Trying To Enter?

Most people assume that the best business idea is one that has absolutely no competition. In most cases, however, your idea will rarely be as unique as you think. There is a high chance that someone else has thought of a similar idea. Even before Zuckerberg started Facebook, there were already social media sites such as Friendster and MySpace. Long before Google came on the scene, there were other search engines, such as Archie, VLib, Veronica, and Infoseek. It is highly unlikely that you will come up with an idea that no one has never thought of before.

Therefore, you want an idea that has some competition in your space. The presence of competition in the space you are trying to enter is validation that there is a demand for your idea. It shows that other people have also identified a problem in that space that needs solving. In addition, the existence of competition also provides you with a roadmap to follow as you seek to grow your business. The lack of competition, on the other hand, could be an indicator that there isn't enough demand in that space.

A simple way to find out if there is competition for your idea is by googling products and services that are similar to what you intend to offer. In addition, you should get out there, talk to your target customers, and find out how they currently solve the problem you are trying to solve. Existing solutions to the problem are the ones provided by your competitors.

If you have concluded that there is some competition in the space you are trying to enter, you are on the right track and can now move to the second question.

**Is The Competition Making Money?**

Just because there are other businesses in the space you are trying to enter does not mean there is money to be made. If all the businesses in that space are struggling, there is a high chance that you will also struggle. To avoid this, you need to find out whether your potential competitors are making money. If they are, this is an indicator that people are willing to pay money to solve the problem you are trying to solve.

There are several ways to find out if your competitors are making money. For instance, you could go through their website and find out if they have earnings announcements. Client success stories and testimonials are also good indicators You can also give them a call, or even walk into their premises (for local businesses) and ask them about s their rates and client experiences. Here I would advise to not mention that you plan to launch a competing business, otherwise you could get dishonest answers.

You can also go through review sites like Yelp to find out what customers are saying about them.

The point here is to find out if your competitors already have customers. If they are successfully selling their products and services, then you are also capable of doing the same, if you have the right approach.

**Beat The Competition**

So far, you have determined that there is a problem that needs solving and that people are willing to pay for the solution. However, this is not a guarantee that they will choose your solution. The only way around this is to make sure your solution beats what is currently available. Customers won't simply buy from you because you have a product. They will only buy if your product is different and better than what the competition is offering. This difference is what defines your Unique Selling Proposition (USP).

There are several ways for your business to stand out from the competition and therefore attract the customers. These include:

- **Come up with something new**: Coming up with a new (and better) way of solving the same problem your competitors are solving is a great way to stand out in a crowded marketplace. For instance, before the launch of the iPhone, there were several mobile phone brands. However, with the iPhone, Apple introduced something totally new: the era of the smartphone. They were still solving the same problem –mobile communication– but they did it in a totally new way, and it's no surprise that they are still at the helm of the smartphone revolution.

- **Lower prices:** Ideally, competing on price is not the best strategy. It is better to provide great value and charge premium prices. However, if you have a way of providing great value and charging low prices for it, while still making good profits, this can be a great way to attract clients. For instance, if you come up with a new production method that allows you to produce at a significantly lower price than the competition, offering lower prices can be a great way to set your product apart.

- **Convenience**: If you can make your products and services more convenient to use compared to what is in the market, this can give you a great advantage over the competition. For instance, before services like Uber and Airbnb existed, there were other companies solving the problems of transportation and accommodation. What companies like Uber and Airbnb brought was convenience, and by doing so, they completely revolutionized and took over those markets.

- **Better quality**: If you had to choose between an iPad and a generic tablet computer from some unknown company, which would you go for? I'm guessing you would go for the iPad. This, because it is from a company that is known for its quality. People love quality products and will go for the highest quality they can get within their budget. Therefore, if you can make your products superior to what the competition is offering–in terms of design, durability, effectiveness–people will be more likely to buy from you.

- **Superior customer service**: Customers are choosing to spend their money on your business, and for this, expect to be treated with respect. Unfortunately, most businesses don't do this. They offer bang average customer service. Luckily for you, this is an advantage. If you can provide excellent customer service, your customers will be happy to ditch the competition and come to you.

- **Offering peace of mind**: For most people, making a purchase is a risk, especially when they are buying from a new, untrusted company. They are spending their money on your products, yet they don't know whether they will like the products, or even whether the products will work as advertised. You can set your business apart by coming up with a way to give your customers peace of mind as they purchase from you. Some ways of doing this include giving money-back guarantees, satisfaction guarantees, offering to replace faulty products, and so on.

If you can answer these questions in the affirmative then you have a valid business idea. You are now certain that your customers have a problem that needs solving, that they are willing to pay for a solution, and that you have a way to incentivize them to buy from you.

You can now go ahead and start preparing a business plan that will transform your business idea into an actual, profitable business. This is what we are going to look at in the next chapter.

# CHAPTER ONE CHECKLIST

Below is a checklist to make sure that you've grasped the key points in the first chapter before moving on to the next. Cross off each point once you fully understand it. Read the chapter once more if necessary.

**Entrepreneurial mindset key points:**

- ☐ Finding my passion
- ☐ Getting comfortable with risk
- ☐ Adopting a goal-oriented attitude
- ☐ Learning to view challenges as opportunities
- ☐ Learning to think strategically
- ☐ Understanding the ecosystem
- ☐ Being driven by your vision
- ☐ Being disciplined

**I understand that in order to come up with great business ideas I can:**

- ☐ Finding problems that need solving
- ☐ Solving future problems
- ☐ Thinking of ways to meet current needs in an ever evolving world
- ☐ Helping people save money
- ☐ Finding a way to make people's lives easier
- ☐ Turning your hobby into a business

**In order to validate my business idea I must ask myself the following 3 questions:**

- ☐ Is there any competition in the space I am trying to enter?
- ☐ Is the competition making money?
- ☐ Do I have a way of making my product, service or idea better?

# 2

# HOW TO CREATE A BUSINESS PLAN

Now that you have come up with a great business idea and validated it, the next step is to create a business plan. This is a very critical step if you want your business to succeed. This is where you get to plan how you will execute your business idea. As the saying goes, failing to plan is planning to fail.

Despite being a very crucial document, a lot of would-be entrepreneurs find it very challenging to come up with a business plan, with some even choosing to start their business without one. Don't be tempted to take that route. In this chapter, I am going to teach you everything you need to know about business plans, including what a business plan is, why you need one, and how to write a great one. I will also give you a template that you can use as a foundation to write your own business plan.

So, what exactly is a business plan?

Like you can probably infer from the two words, a business plan is simply a plan for your business. It is a document that acts as a roadmap for your business. It describes how your business is going to work, outlines the goals and objectives of your business, as well as the detailed plans that will help your business achieve these goals and objectives. In a nutshell, it is simply a guide on how you are going to make your business succeed.

## WHY DO YOU NEED A BUSINESS PLAN?

There are several reasons why you need to come up with a business plan before launching your business. Some of these include:

**To Secure Funding**

This is perhaps the most popular reason (but not the most important) behind writing a business plan. Actually, some people believe that the sole purpose of a business plan is to help entrepreneurs secure funding.

In most cases, new businesses will require some startup capital to get things rolling. Sometimes, however, the business owner might not have the money required to start the business. In such cases, the entrepreneur will have to rely on debt or equity financing from financiers and investors.

With the high rate of business failure, investors and financiers want to be sure they are putting their money into a venture that will be profitable, not something that will go under soon after and drag down their money with it. The business plan provides them with a tool to evaluate the feasibility of the business before they decide to invest in it.

Without a business plan, your chances of securing funds to start your new business are next to nil. Therefore, if you are considering borrowing some money to fund your new business, you need to develop a business plan.

**For Planning Purposes**

This is the main purpose of a business plan. Creating a business plan helps you to think about everything that is required to make your business a success. It will help you plan the best way to solve your customers' problem, how to promote and market your products and services, how to win market share from the competition, the time you need to get to certain milestones, the resources you need to get your business off the ground, and so on. As you write your business plan, you will also be able to identify potential problems you might encounter. All this will make your startup journey a lot smoother and increase your chances of success. A 2010 study on business planning by Andrew Burke, Stuart Fraser, and Francis Greene, which was published in the *Journal of Management Studies,* found that companies with business plans grow 30% faster than those without.

**To Know If Your Idea is Feasible**

Just because you have a business idea that is profitable doesn't mean that you will achieve success. It all depends on how you execute the idea. To know if your execution plan is feasible, you have two options. The first one is to launch the business and hope everything works. This is a very expensive and time-consuming way of finding the feasibility of your idea. The second option is to create a business plan to test the feasibility of your execution plan. The process of creating a business plan will reveal whether or not there are any flaws in your execution plan. This will save you a lot of time and money, which you would have lost if you launched without a business plan.

## For Research Purposes

To come up with a business plan, you will need to conduct lots of research. Research about your ideal customer, research about the size of the market and market trends, research about your competitors, and so on. This information is very important since it will help you come up with strategies to ensure the success of your business.

## Ease The Partnership Process

In the event that you decide to approach other businesses for collaboration and partnerships, it is important for both of you to be on the same page before embarking on a partnership. Your business plan will provide your potential partner with a clear overview of your business objectives, your audience, your vision, and your strategies for growth. This information will be useful in helping your potential partner to determine if your business is a good fit for them, especially if you are trying to partner with a business that is bigger than yours.

## To counterbalance your emotions

Running a business is an emotionally charged affair. Sometimes, your passion for your business and your ideas might drive you to make unrealistic assumptions. Sometimes, you might be overwhelmed with fear or self-doubt. In some cases, these strong emotions might get the best of you and this could result in rash decisions that could be detrimental for your business. However, when you have a business plan that outlines what you need to do and for what purpose, you are less likely to make irrational and emotion-based decisions.

## HOW TO WRITE A BUSINESS PLAN

Contrary to popular belief, drawing up a business plan is quite easy. However, you will need to dedicate time and effort to carry out the needed research for various sections of your business plan. While there are different kinds of business plans, depending on the nature of the business you intend to start, there are some key elements that are found in most business plans.

### The Executive Summary

This is usually the first part of a business plan. The executive summary provides a quick overview of what is contained in the rest of the business plan. It gives an outline of your business, what you do, who you are targeting, and some key financial highlights.

The aim of the executive summary is to give readers without a lot of time (such as potential investors) the big picture of your business. Ideally, the executive summary should be able to stand on its own. It should be very clear and concise, highlighting all the key aspects of your business, but without going into too much detail. You can think of it as a one-page business plan. Some investors will only ask for your executive summary, rather than the whole business plan.

If they like the information presented in the executive summary, they might then ask for something to shed more light on your business, such as a pitch presentation, a complete business plan, or more detailed financial information. Therefore, you need to make sure that your executive summary is intriguing and compelling. However, if your business does not require financing or partnerships and you are only writing a business plan for your own purposes, you can leave out the executive summary.

Even though the executive summary is the first chapter of your business plan, it is recommended that you write it last, after you have written the rest of the business plan. This way, you will have a clear idea of what is contained in the rest of the business plan. Remember, the executive summary is, just as it sounds, a summary of your business plan.

Ideally, your executive summary should be about one page in length. Below are some of the things that the executive summary should cover:

- **Problem Summary**: An overview of the problem you are trying to solve for your customers. This is basically a justification for why your business needs to exist.
- **Solution Summary**: An overview of what your business does, its products and services, and how they are different from what is in the market.
- **Target Market**: A brief overview of the market segment you are targeting.
- **Competition**: An overview of your key competition.
- **Marketing Plan**: A brief summary of how you intend to reach your customers.
- **Current Financial State**: A brief overview of your company's current financial status.
- **Financial Forecasts**: A brief overview of the

financial targets you intend to hit in the next
6 months, 1 year, or 2 years.

- **Financing Needed**: If the aim of your
  business plan is to secure funding, give a
  brief overview of the amount of money you
  need. If you aren't trying to secure funding,
  leave out this part.
- **Why Us**: A brief overview of the people
  involved in running the business and why
  they are the right people to run this business.

**The Opportunity**

This is the first chapter of a business plan. This is
where you go into detail about the problem you are
trying to solve, how you are solving it, the market
segment you are targeting, how your product fits
into the market, who your competition is and how
you will deal with them, and so on. This chapter
should contain the following sections:

- **The Problem Worth Solving:** In this
  section, you will define the problem that
  your business will solve for its customers.
  Here, you will need to answer questions such
  as what your customers' primary pain point
  is? What are the existing solutions for this

pain point? Why do you feel that the existing solutions are not effective? To be able to properly define the problem, you will need to go out there and talk to potential customers. What you think is their greatest problem might actually not be a problem. The only way to validate your assumptions is to talk to them.

- **The Solution:** In this section, you should go into the details of how you intend to solve the problem you identified above. What are your products or services? How do they solve the problem? Why are they better at solving the problem compared to what is in the market?

- **Target Market**: After defining the problem and describing your solution, the next thing is to explain who you intend to sell to. Here, avoid the temptation to describe your target market as everyone. Just because you have a product that can be potentially used by everyone doesn't mean that everyone will be willing to buy it. Identify the group of people for whom the problem you are trying to solve is a real pain point. Having a good idea of who your target market is will help you come up with the right sales processes and marketing campaigns.

- **Market Research:** Don't just stop at describing who your target market is. Go a step further and conduct some research into how big the market is and the different segments within that market. This will help you to determine if the market is big enough to support the success of your business.

- **Market Trends:** In this section, you are going to describe the notable changes that are happening in your target market. Are there any significant changes in the needs and preferences of your potential customers? Is there a new market segment that is starting to gain interest in the kind of products or services you are offering? How do you intend to take advantage of these changes to give your business an edge?

- **Market Growth:** In this section, you will explain the growth your target market has undergone over the last couple of years. Is it growing or shrinking? If the market is growing, this is a good sign, since it shows that there is an increasing demand for solutions to the problem you are trying to solve. If the market is shrinking, this is not a very encouraging sign, though it is still possible to be successful in such a market. However, you will need to understand that you are swimming against the current. To find out the kind of growth happening in your target market, you will need to carry out a lot of research.

- **Competition**: In this section, you will describe who your key competitors are. To determine who your competitors are, you should think of the various ways through which your customers currently solve the problem you are trying to solve. Here, even businesses that do not seem to be direct competitors could still be in competition with you. For instance, if you are launching a beer brand, you might assume that your only competition is other beer brands and alcoholic drinks. However, if someone is sitting in a restaurant waiting for some- one, a question like this might go through their mind: should I drink a beer or soda? Because both your beer and soda are solving the same problem (the customer needs something to drink), they are both in competition, albeit indirectly. Apart from describing your competition, you should also describe which competitive advantages you have that will help you gain a chunk of the market share. Do you have access to new technology that your competitors do not? Do you have some intellectual property rights that make your product or service superior?

**Execution**

This is the second chapter of your business plan. This is where you will go into the details about how you will make your business work. In this chapter, you are going to cover things such as how you will sell and market your products, how your business will operate, how you will measure success, and so on. This chapter will include the following sections:

- **Marketing Plan**: Here, you are going to describe the strategies that you will employ to reach your target market, as well as how you intend to position your business and your products and services in the market. Your chosen strategies will depend on your ideal customer. For instance, if your ideal customer spends more time on Instagram than Facebook, then part of your marketing plan will include Instagram marketing. Your marketing plan should include details such as your pricing plan, and the reason why you decided to price your products that way, your positioning statement, which explains how you will position your products and company to differentiate yourself in the market, and your promotion strategies, including the reasons why these strategies are the best suited for your target customers.

- **Sales Plan**: This will describe how you will get your customers to buy your products and services. Mention any sales channels and processes you have in place, the people who will be in charge of selling your products, as well as the place where you will sell your products.

- **Operations**: This section details how your business will operate. Here, you will need to describe things such as the people or companies that will supply you with the raw materials you require for production, the locations and facilities where your products will be produced, and how you will get the products to the customers. If you are not manufacturing your own products, describe how you will get the products, whether this is through partnering with wholesalers or through dropshipping. You should also describe all matters to do with your inventory, such as how much inventory you intend to maintain, where this inventory will be stored, how you will monitor and track inventory, and how you will deal with unexpected spikes in demand and busy seasons. If you have some technology that will play a key role in the operation of your business, describe it and how it works. The point here is to show the reader that you have a pretty clear idea of how your business will work and of your supply chain, and that you have solid plans in place to deal with potential uncertainties. If you are writing the business plan for yourself, the operations plan will help you make key decisions about your business, such as how to reduce costs, how to price your products, how to plan your break-even point, and so on.

- **Milestones And Metrics**: For a plan to be useful, you need to break it into steps that you need to follow while implementing the plan. In this section, you will describe the steps that you need to take, the dates before which the steps need to be completed, as well as the people responsible for each of these steps. In addition, you will also describe the key metrics that you will use to monitor and keep track of how your business is growing. Examples of metrics that you might want to monitor include the number of leads generated, sales, website visitors or any other metric that will give you a good idea of how your business is growing. The milestones and metrics section does not need to be overly long. The point is to make it clear what steps need to be taken to make your business successful.

- **Key Assumptions And Risks:** Here, you are going to describe the key assumptions you have made that are crucial for the success of your business, both favorable and unfavorable. For instance, if the success of your business depends heavily on Instagram marketing, you are making the assumption that Instagram will always be a great platform for marketing. If Instagram were to shut down a few months down the line, this would pose a huge threat to your business. The good thing with knowing your key assumptions and risks is that it allows you to prepare. If you know your key assumptions, you will focus on proving if they are correct. The aim is to minimize assumptions and therefore remove any uncertainties from your business. Similarly, when you know the risks you might face, you will start developing contingencies before these risks become actual problems.

## The Company

This is the third chapter of your business plan. This chapter provides an overview of your company, including the structure and the people involved with running it. If you are writing the business plan for your own use, you have the option of leaving out this chapter. It is usually the shortest chapter in the business plan, and consists of the following sections:

- **Company Overview**: In this section, you are going to describe the ownership of the company, its legal structure (sole proprietorship, incorporated company, limited partnership, or general partnership), a brief history of the company and why it was founded, as well as its location. You are also going to include information such as the mission and vision, the company's values, any intellectual property held by the company, the nature of the business, the industry in which the company is operating, and your business objectives.

- **The Team**: In this section, you will give a list of all the key members involved in the running of the business, a brief bio of these team members, as well as an explanation as to why these people are the right people for these roles. Most businesses succeed or fail depending on the those who are tasked with running them. Moreover, investors will want to know the people behind the company and their qualifications before putting money into the business. Even if you are writing the business plan for your own use, this section can help you discover any oversight in the team tasked with running the business.

**Financial Plan**

This is the final chapter of your business plan. This chapter is crucial because running a successful business involves paying close attention to your income and expenditure. Having a solid financial plan will help you make key decisions like deciding when you can purchase new equipment, when to bring in new employees, when to expand the business, and so on. If you are trying to secure funding from investors or financiers, a good financial plan will also help you determine how much money you need to get your business off the ground, which will, in turn, help you determine how much money to borrow.

This chapter consists of the following sections:

- **Sales Forecast:** In this section, you are going to provide projections or estimates about the number of sales you expect to make over the next two or three years. You don't have to go into too much detail at this point. Just provide a high-level overview of how much you expect to sell. If your business has multiple products or services, you should provide projections for each product or service separately.

- **Personnel Plan**: In this section, you will go into the details of employee salaries. If you are starting a small business, you can create a list of all the people you intend to hire and the amount of money you are going to pay each of them every month. For a big company, this might not be feasible. What needs to be done in this case is a break-down of the personnel plan by departments, such as "sales," "finance" and "IT." You are also going to include the employee burden in this section. Employee burden refers to other costs that come with having employees on your payroll other than salary. This might include things such as insurance and taxes.

- **Profit And Loss Statement**: Also referred to

as an income statement, this is a document that brings together all your numbers and helps you determine whether you are making or losing money. The income statement includes all your sources of revenue within a given period (extracted from your sales forecast) and your expenses over the same period (personnel costs, production costs, and all other expected expenses). The income statement gives a bottom line by subtracting the expenses from the revenue, and helps you determine whether you are going to be making profits or incurring losses.

- **Cash Flow Statement:** The cash flow statement is almost similar to the income statement, and sometimes even gets confused with the income statement. Just like the income statement, the cash flow statement consists of a list of your revenue and your expenses. However, there is one key difference between the two. Whereas the income statement will include revenue from all sales within a certain period, and all expenses from the same period, the cash flow statement also takes into consideration when your company collects revenue, and when it pays out its expenses. As a result, it is a great tool for keeping track of the amount of cash that the business has at hand at a certain time. Unlike the income statement, the cash flow statement does not calculate profit and loss. By keeping track of the amount of cash you have at hand, the cash flow statement helps you to determine when you have surplus money, or when you have low amounts of cash and might need to borrow money to keep your business running. Since your business is still new and money has not yet started flowing, you should create a projected cash flow statement for the next twelve months.

- **Balance Sheet:** This is a financial statement that gives you a look into the financial health of your company. The balance sheet consists of a list of all the assets owned by your business (equity) and a list of what you owe (liabilities). Subtracting the total liabilities from total assets will help you determine how much your business is worth.

BUSINESS PLAN TEMPLATE

To make it easier for you to create a business plan below is a template that you can use as a foundation.

**[Company Name]**
*[Tagline]*

**Business Plan**
[Date]

**Contact Information**
[Telephone]
[Email]
[Website]
[Address]

TABLE OF CONTENTS

**Executive Summary:**

**Opportunity:**

**Execution:**

**The Company:**

**Financial Plan:**

## EXECUTIVE SUMMARY


**Target market**:

**Competition**:

**Marketing Plan**:

**Current financial state**:

**Financial forecasts**:

**Financing needed**:

**Why us**:


## CHAPTER ONE: OPPORTUNITY:


**Problem Worth Solving**

**The Solution**

**Target Market**

**Market Research**

**Market Trends**

**Market Growth**

**Competition**

CHAPTER TWO: EXECUTION:

**Marketing Plan**
**Sales Plan**
**Operations**
**Milestones And Metrics**
**Key Assumptions And Risks**

CHAPTER THREE: THE COMPANY:

**Company Overview**
**The Team**

CHAPTER FOUR: FINANCIAL PLAN:

**Sales Forecast**
[insert tables or charts to show sales projections]
**Personnel Plan**
[insert tables and charts to show salaries and
employee burden]
**Profit And Loss Statement**

[insert profit and loss statement]

**Cash Flow Statement**

[insert cash flow statement]

**Balance Sheet**

[insert balance sheet]

Below is a handy checklist you can use when writing your business plan.

**My executive summary has the following sections:**

- ☐ Problem Summary
- ☐ Solution Summary
- ☐ Target Market
- ☐ Competition
- ☐ Marketing Plan
- ☐ Current Financial State
- ☐ Financial Forecasts
- ☐ Financing Needed
- ☐ Why Us

**The opportunity chapter of my business plan has the following sections:**

- ☐ Problem Worth Solving
- ☐ The Solution
- ☐ Target Market
- ☐ Market Research
- ☐ Market Trends
- ☐ Market Growth
- ☐ Competition

**The execution chapter of my business plan has the following sections:**

- ☐ Marketing Plan
- ☐ Sales Plan
- ☐ Operations
- ☐ Milestones And Metrics
- ☐ Key Assumptions And Risks

**The company chapter of my business plan has the following sections:**

- ☐ Company Overview
- ☐ The Team

**The financial plan chapter of my business plan has the following sections:**

☐ Sales Forecast

☐ Personnel Plan

☐ Profit And Loss Statement

☐ Cash Flow Statement

☐ Balance Sheet

# 3

# MANAGING FINANCES AND FUNDING

A s you've heard many times, it takes money to make money. To get your new business up and running, you need access to money, usually referred to as start-up capital or seed money. This is the money that will be used to pay for leasing office space, buying necessary equipment, acquiring necessary licenses and permits, hiring your first workers, producing your products or acquiring inventory, marketing, and all other expenses associated with starting a new business.

In an ideal world, an entrepreneur will have enough money saved up to fund their new business. Even though some entrepreneurs do fund their new ventures with nothing other than their personal savings, this isn't the case for everyone. Starting a new business, as any logical individual would know, requires money. So, how do you finance your business if you're starting from zero?

Below are several approaches you can use to raise start-up capital:

**Borrow Money From Friends And Family**

This is a very common way of raising startup capital, and also one of the easiest. According to a joint study by the Kauffman Foundation and Babson College, London Business School, 70% of all capital investments in start-ups comes from friends and family.

With this approach, you simply need to talk to some of your friends and family, tell them about your business idea, and ask them to loan you some money to fund the idea. The best part about this approach is that you won't be asked to fill endless paperwork or go miles to prove the viability of your business idea.

While it is the easiest, this approach is also one of the riskiest. If you get start-up capital from your friends and family and your business fails (which is a possibility for every new business), you will not only be risking your loved ones' financial future, you will also be risking your personal relationship with them.

The best approach when asking for startup capital from friends and family is to treat it with the same seriousness you would when borrowing money from an investor. Go over your business plan with them and show them your projections to provide evidence that you are not just sinking their money into a stupid venture. Clearly state the terms of the arrangement (is it a loan or an equity investment?), and how you intend to repay. Finally, remind them that there is risk involved, and that they could potentially lose their money.

**Get A Bank Loan**

This is another common way of raising startup capital. While the restrictions on lending are much tighter nowadays, there are still a lot of banks and financial institutions that will lend you money to fund your startup if you can convince them that you have a viable business idea.

The process of applying for a bank loan will take you about two to three months, therefore you need to factor this when planning your business launch. The bank will require you to provide sufficient documentation about your venture, and you should be prepared to answer lots of questions about it and your personal financial situation. Before applying for a bank loan, you also need to make sure that you have a good credit rating, since this is something the bank will put into consideration before approving your application.

In some cases, you might be asked to provide collateral or personal guarantee for the bank loan. For instance, you might be asked to pledge your equipment, your house, your accounts receivables, and so on. While this will increase your chances of getting approved for the loan, you should weigh your options carefully to limit your exposure. For instance, in case the business fails, it is much better to lose your equipment than your house.

**Find Angel Investors**

This approach involves finding investors with money, and getting them to buy into your idea either as a loan or most typically, in exchange for equity. Angel investors are in it for the money, therefore, you need to show them that your idea will indeed be profitable.

If you want to increase your chances of getting

money from angel investors, make sure you know your stuff. You should be armed with a business plan, sales and marketing plans, market research, competitor analysis, and so on. You need to make them confident in your business' viability. Having experienced people on your management team can also increase investor confidence and your chances of getting funds from angel investors.

Very often, angel investors will opt to invest in business with some demonstrated value rather than abstract ideas. In that case, even if they don't buy into your idea right away, don't give up. Keep in touch with them, and periodically update them on the progress your business is making. Seeing some progress might allay their fears and convince them to invest in your company's growth.

**Use A Credit Card**

Credit cards are another easy way of raising money to fund your new business. According to a survey by Arthur Andersen and the National Small Business Association, about half of all small business owners have at one point used their credit cards to fund their business' formation or expansion. Used responsibly, credit cards can be a great way to pad your finances when your cash flow is low.

Unfortunately, with ease comes risk. Credit cards have some of the highest interest rates, and if you are not careful, using credit cards to fund your startup could land you in a hole of debt that might take you years to get out of. Aside from the high interest rates, the penalties are numerous and high if you miss any payments.

If you decide to use credit cards to fund your business, have separate cards for personal and business expenses. The credit card interest charged on business expenses is tax deductible, and keeping your personal and business expenses separate will make it easy for you to claim these deductions.

**Use Funds From Your 401(k)**

Many people are not aware of this, but you can actually use the money in your 401(k) to fund your business. To do this, however, you need to follow the right procedure, otherwise you might face hefty penalties.

Tapping into your 401(k) to fund your business involves some legal complexities, including setting up a C corporation that has a retirement fund into which your retirement assets can be rolled. To avoid falling on the wrong side of the law, it is advisable to have a CPA, a tax attorney, or someone well versed with establishing C corporations handle this for you. The person should also be highly knowledgeable about the Employee Retirement Income Security Act (ERISA).

When funding your new business using the funds in your 401(k), don't forget that you are taking a double risk. If the business fails, you lose the business as well as your retirement nest egg. Therefore, it is advisable to minimize your risk by not using all your retirement funds.

**Crowdfund Your Business**

The ubiquity of the internet has led to the growth of unconventional ways of raising funds for a new business. Crowdfunding is one of them. With crowdfunding, you basically pitch your business idea to people on the internet, let them know how much money you need, and then ask them to contribute money to your idea. If they like your idea, people will give you money to implement it, in exchange for something, such as getting your product once your business is up and running.

There are several sites where you can crowdsource money to fund your idea. The most popular is Kick-starter.com. Ever since its inception in 2009, Kick-starter has successfully funded over 176,000 projects and raised over $4.7 billion. Other popular crowdfunding sites include Indiegogo and GoFundMe. GoFundMe is more geared towards social causes and unfortunate life events, but you can still find people to fund your business idea on the site.

If you want to raise enough money for your start-up through crowdfunding, you need to tap into your social network. Remember, there are thousands of other projects vying for the same crowdfunding dollars as you, and therefore, your chances of hitting your target are higher when you rally up strong support from your followers on social media. This means that you will need to do some marketing to get more people to support your idea.

**Get An SBA Loan**

The US Small Business Administration (SBA) is a government agency that provides guarantees for loans by financial institutions to small businesses that cannot ordinarily access loans from these financial institutions. The SBA itself does not offer loans. Instead, it guarantees the lender that it will pay the loans in case the small business is unable to pay the loan.

There are some conditions that you need to meet in order to qualify for an SBA loan. These include:

- You need to have applied for a loan from a financial institution and got turned down. The SBA only guarantees small businesses that cannot obtain loans on their own.
- Your business needs to fit the government's definition of a small business. This definition will vary depending on the industry you are operating in. Some industries are judged based on number of employees, others on annual income, and so on.
- Your business will need to meet other qualification requirements based on the type of loan you are applying for.
- After meeting the above conditions, you will need to apply for a loan from a bank or financial institution that offers SBA loans. Remember, the SBA doesn't offer loans itself. You will need to pass the bank's qualification requirements in order to be approved for the loan.

Below are some things you need to do to increase your chances of qualifying for an SBA loan:

- Make sure you have a good credit score, preferably in the high 700s and above.
- Have a business plan ready, detailing what business you want to get into, why you need money, and how you will ensure the success of the business.
- If you are borrowing money to fund the growth of an existing business, you will need to have a complete financial history of your business. However, since you are starting a new business, this is not necessary.
- Have financial projections ready to show that your business's ability to pay back the loan.

**Get A Microloan**

Microloans are small business loans offered by micro lenders. Microloans typically range between $500 and $35,000. The good thing with micro lenders is that they give loans that are way smaller than banks would give you, have more flexible underwriting criteria, and don't need as much documentation as banks. A microloan can be the perfect way to fund your business idea if you are unable to raise funds through a bank loan.

Microloans have several advantages, including:

- They give very small loan amounts, so you don't have to borrow more than you need. This will also get you used to making debt payments before you start borrowing bigger amounts to expand your business.
- Microloans usually have very flexible repayment terms.
- Micro lenders will often play the role of advisors. Before giving you the loan, they will want to understand your business and might offer help with things such as drafting business plans and coming up with better sales and marketing plans.
- Micro lenders will often give you loans even if your credit score is not perfect.

Despite all these advantages, microloans also have some downsides, including:

- Micro lenders charge significantly higher interest rates compared to banks. Still, they are cheaper than other ways of raising funds, such as credit card loans.

- Microloans are, by definition, small loans. Therefore, if your business needs a lot of capital to get running, microloans might not work for you.

## HOW TO KEEP GOOD FINANCIAL RECORDS AND KEEP YOUR BUSINESS ORGANIZED

Once you have raised enough capital and have finally gotten your business up and running, you will need to properly manage these funds and make sure they are being put to the right use. One of the best and most effective ways of doing this is to keep good financial records.

A lot of new business owners ignore record keeping, either because they find it hard, or do not know the importance of keeping business records. However, as many later come to find out, keeping good financial records is a very crucial aspect of running a business.

Below are some reasons why keeping proper financial records is very important, according to the IRS:

- **Monitoring your business:** Records help you monitor how your business is progressing. You can tell whether your business is growing or not, which products you need to put greater focus on, which products you should stop selling, and so on. Your business is more likely to succeed when you keep proper records.

- **Preparing financial statements**: Preparing accurate financial statement –such as income statements and balance sheets–is impossible when you don't have proper records. These financial statements are very useful in helping you manage your business and helping you deal with your creditors.

- **Identifying income sources:** When you run a business, money will come from multiple sources. Proper record keeping will help you identify where the money is coming from. This, in turn, will help you separate nontaxable income from taxable income.

- **Tracking deductible expenses**: Many business expenses are tax deductible, but without a proper record of these expenses, you won't be able to remember all of them when filing your tax returns.

- **Preparation of tax returns**: Good records are very crucial when it comes to filing tax returns. With proper records, you will have an accurate idea of your income and expenses. Having proper records will also support whatever you report when filing your tax returns, in case the IRS needs to further examine your returns.

While many business owners view record keeping as a pain in the neck, it doesn't have to be so. Below are some tips that will make the task a lot easier for you.

**Buy Good Accounting Software**

While you can keep records the old fashioned way–writing them down on a ledger book–it is far much better and easier to use an accounting software. Luckily, there is no shortage of accounting software. If your budget is too tight, you can use spreadsheet software like MS Excel or Google Spreadsheets to keep your records, but if you have the money for it, I would advise purchasing professional accounting software such as QuickBooks, FreshBooks, or Zoho Books. Here, you can either go for desktop based or online software. I recommend going for an online version of the accounting software of your choice.

Online software is much cheaper, has no upgrade cost, allows you to access your files from anywhere, and minimises the risk of losing files.

**Set Up Bank Accounts For Your Business**

One of the biggest mistakes most new business owners make is using their personal bank account for their business. Doing so makes it very difficult to distinguish personal activities and expenses from business activities and expenses. Tracking business income and expenses becomes a challenge, not to mention the nightmare you are going to have when it comes to filing your taxes.

To avoid this, create a separate bank account for your business. This will make it easy for you to keep track of your business income and expenditure. You should also note that for corporations, partnerships, and LLCs, having a separate bank account is a legal requirement.

When creating a bank account for your business, it is advisable to shop for a bank that is willing to give you credit to fund your business expansion when the time comes.

**Avoid Using Cash**

The problem with cash is that it doesn't leave any paper trail. Cash payments with no corresponding receipt can be hard to remember when it is time to take an account of your expenses..

Instead of using cash, get in the habit of using a credit or debit card for all your business expenses. This way, there will be proper documentation to help with tracking expenses. This will also make it easy for you to claim tax deductible expenses, since there is documented proof of these expenses.

**Save All Receipts**

Whenever you incur a business expense, make sure to save the receipt from that transaction. If they are physical receipts, have a file folder you keep them in. If they are electronic receipts emailed to your, create a receipts folder in your email. The point here is that you should be able to provide appropriate documentation for all your business expenses.

**Have A Specific Time For Updating Your Records**

To ensure that no transaction goes unrecorded, you should have a scheduled time for updating your records. This can either be at the end of each business day, or at the end of the week. With such a schedule, it is unlikely that you will forget updating some records. Regularly updating your records also allows you to keep on top of your business' progress.

**Tax Obligations**

Keep a record of all your tax obligations to ensure you have a clear picture of what you need to remit to the IRS and when. For instance, if you have employees, you will need to keep track of the amount of PAYE you need to remit. Similarly, if you sell goods that are subject to VAT, you need to keep track of the amount you need to remit as VAT. Fortunately, having a professional accounting software can automate all this for you.

**Maintain A Record Of All Your Accounting Documents**

Your business is required by law to keep the following documents and make them available upon request:

- Bank account statements.
- Invoices and receipts for goods sold or services rendered by your business.
- Invoices and receipts for goods or services procured by your business.
- Business tax return documents.

- Credit card statements.
- Payroll records, as well as submitted payroll tax deductions.
- All financial statements – income statements, cash flow statements, and balance sheets.

## Hire A Bookkeeper

If you find it hard to keep proper records by yourself, or if your business has grown so much that you are unable to keep good financial records by yourself, it is advisable to hire an experienced bookkeeper to handle this for you. In addition to making sure that your business records are in proper hands, hiring a bookkeeper will also free you up to focus on other aspects of the business.

## Keeping Track Of Your Expenses And Income

To keep track of expenses and income in your new business, you need to learn to stay on top of your cash flow. As discussed in the previous chapter, cash flow keeps track of the total amount of money coming into your business, and the total amount of money going out your business within a given period. All the money coming into the business is referred to as income. This includes payments from clients, bank loans, and so on. All the money going out of the business is referred to as expenses, and includes payments to employees, rent payments, money used on business travel, money spent on marketing, and so on.

Staying on top of your business' cash flow is important because it allows you to determine whether your business is profitable (when income is greater than expenses) or not. Sometimes, your business' expenses will be greater than your income. This is especially common for a new business, since you might not have started making enough sales, yet keeping the business running involves various expenses.

Regardless of whether you have started making sales or not, you need to track your expenses and income right from the moment you open up for business. Let's take a look at how to do this.

TRACKING YOUR INCOME

**Issue Professional Invoices:** The invoice is one of the most important documents when it comes to tracking your income. The invoice keep a record of a sale, noting the sale amount, the paid amount, and any pending balance. It also keeps a record of when a pending payment is due, and is useful for following up when the payment is due.

To ensure that all your sales are recorded and paid on time, you should make sure that each sale is accompanied by an invoice that has a date, an invoice number (unique number for identifying the invoice), a description of the goods or services sold, the client's purchase order number (this shows that procurement of your goods or services was preapproved and minimizes delay of payment), your business' contact information, the total cost of the sale, and the payment terms (when is the payment due?).

**Create A Profit And Loss Report:** This is a financial document that details the total revenue your business earned within a certain period, and the expenses it incurred within the same period. Subtracting the expenses from the revenue gives you the profit for that period. The profit and loss report is an important tool for helping a business better manage its future spending. For instance, if your profits are low because you are paying a lot on rent, you know your business needs to find cheaper business premises.

**Tracking Your Expenses**

This is something that a lot of new business owners find challenging, but with the right approach, it is not a difficult thing to do. Below are tips on how to track your business expenses:

- **Set up a business bank account:** I already mentioned the importance of having a separate bank account for your business. Paying for all your business expenses from this account makes it easy to keep track of where your money is going. Seeing as you will be making a lot of transactions from this account, it is advisable to go for a bank that has minimal transaction charges.

- **Put your expenses into categories:** It is not enough to know how much expenses you are incurring, you also need to know where the money is going. Knowing where your money is going can help you determine where you need to cut costs. To know where your money is going (and how much is going there), put your expenses into categories like payroll, rent, phone and utilities, office supplies, marketing and advertising expenses, travel expenses, professional services, and so on. Having a good understanding of how much you spend on each category will help you determine where most of your money is going, where you are spending without any significant returns, and where you need to boost spending to increase revenue.

- **Track your expenses by client:** Depending on the nature of your business, there might be costs associated with maintaining your clients. What you might not be aware of, however, is that some clients could be more expensive to maintain than others. Tracking your expenses by client will help you to determine which clients are expensive to maintain, and whether their business is worth the expenses you spend on them. You might discover that a certain client costs you too much, with little returns. In such a case, you can choose to cut off the client or revise your pricing for such a client.

Below is a checklist to further help you manage your business finances.

**I am going to use the following methods to raise money to fund my new business:**

☐ Borrow money from friends and family

☐ Get a bank loan

☐ Find an angel investors

☐ Use my credit card

☐ Use funds from my 401(k)

☐ Seek crowdfunding

☐ Get an SBA loan

☐ Get a microloan

**I have done/will do the following to ensure I keep good records and my business organized:**

- ☐ Bought good accounting software
- ☐ Set up bank accounts for my business
- ☐ Stopped using cash
- ☐ Started saving all receipts
- ☐ Have scheduled a specific time for updating my records
- ☐ Started keeping a record of all my tax obligations
- ☐ Started maintaining a record of all my accounting documents
- ☐ Hired a bookkeeper

**I have done/will do the following to keep track of expenses and profits in my new business:**

- ☐ Issue professional invoices
- ☐ Create profit and loss reports
- ☐ Set up a business bank account
- ☐ Put my business expenses into categories
- ☐ Track my expenses by client

# 4

# SELL YOURSELF TO CUSTOMERS

K nowing how to sell your products and services is a skill you cannot do without. You might have the best product in the market, you might be offering the lowest prices, you might have the best customer service, but if you don't know how to sell, none of that matters because you are not going to make a dime.

Knowing how to sell is especially important today where the customer holds much of the power in making a purchasing decision. The internet has made it possible for buyers to conveniently research just about any product before making a purchase decision. Therefore, marketing and selling techniques that worked in the past might not be so effective today.

The key to effectively selling your products and services lies in knowing who your customers are, understanding their needs and preferences, knowing where they are carrying out their research before making their purchase decisions, and knowing the factors that influence their decision. Once you know this, customize your marketing and selling strategies to match your customers' behaviors and preferences.

In this chapter, we are going to look at the three important aspects of selling yourself to customers: conducting market research, marketing your business, and closing more sales.

## CARRYING OUT MARKET RESEARCH

Market research refers to the process through which you gather information about your customers, their behaviors, their needs and preferences, what they are looking for, and the things that might influence them to buy your products or services. The aim of market research is to determine how suited your products and services are to these people, and the best ways to get them to know about and purchase your products and services.

Market research allows you to find out the trends in

your industry, as well as alternative products that your customers might opt for. This is important because it will help you figure out how to differentiate your products from what is in the market.

If done well, market research will help you to:

- Better identify the specific niches that are most likely to be interested in your products and services.
- Create engaging marketing materials that are likely to resonate with your target market.
- Come up with ideas for new products and services based on your customers' wants and needs.
- Reduce the likelihood of positioning your products and services poorly.
- Identify changes in consumer behavior and adapt to these changes early.
- Identify industry trends before they become mainstream and make adjustments to take advantage of them.

When carrying out market research, you should be trying to answer the following questions:

- **Who are your customers?** Before trying to understand what your customers are looking for or how they make their purchase decisions, the first thing you need to do is to understand who your customers are. Here, the aim is to define the buyer persona of your ideal customer and gain a good understanding of the characteristics that describe them. Try to understand the age of your ideal customer, their gender, where they live, the kind of work they do, their job titles, marital status, family size, income, the places where you are likely to find them (both online and offline), their challenges, why they are looking for a solution to the problem you are trying to solve, their greatest influences when making their purchase decisions, and so on. The more you know about your ideal customer, the easier it becomes to sell to them. For instance, if you are in the car sales business, the way you sell to a 55-year-old man is not the same way you will to a 27-year-old man. These two men live in different places, they probably have very different kinds of jobs, their family size is totally different, their incomes are different, they hangout in different places (both online and offline), they are influenced by different things, have different preferences, and need a car for totally different reasons.

- **What products are they using now?** Here, you want to understand your ideal customers' current buying habits in relation to the product or service you are trying to sell. Understand how much they spend, how often they buy, where they prefer buying, the features they love most, and so on.

- **Why do they buy?** With this question, you are trying to understand the motivation behind their purchase decisions. Of course, the answers to this question will depend on what you are selling, and who you are selling it to. Going back to the automobile example, the 55-year-old might buy a car because it has enough space for a big family, enough room in the trunk, and can handle terrain outside the city. The 27-year-old, on the other hand, will probably buy a car because it looks cool or because it is fast.

- **Why would they buy from me?** With this question, you are trying to find out the advantages your products and services have over the competition from the perspective of your customers. Do they have unresolved pain points that you can help with?

The better you can answer these questions, the easier you will find it to market yourself and sell to your customers.

There are two types of market research: primary research and secondary research.

## Primary Research

This refers to the process where a business or entrepreneur gathers information directly from the market. It refers to the acquisition of firsthand information. Conducting primary research is very useful when you are trying to establish your buyers' persona and segment your market.

You can conduct primary research through a number of ways, including:

- **Online surveys**: These are particularly useful when you want to reach a huge number of people quickly and in a cost-effective manner. It is very effective for collecting market feedback.

- **Telephone surveys**: These are great for conducting in-depth interviews and gathering feedback from current or prospective customers in the B2B environment. The downside is that many people are wary of answering such calls or participating in telephone surveys.

- **Direct mail surveys**: These are useful when you want to get feedback from a geographically distributed sample of respondents. However, they take a long time and the response rates are excruciatingly low.

- **Focus groups**: Focus groups involve bringing together current or potential customers and asking them to share their feelings about the market or a particular product. They are very useful for gaining in-depth insights into customer tastes and preferences.

- **Face-to-face interviews**: This involves talking to people in person and finding out what they feel about the market or a product. You can talk to friends and family, people shopping for similar products to what you sell, random people, and so on.

- **Observation**: This involves passively observing the behaviors of prospective customers when shopping for or interacting with a product. This method is useful for understanding customer behavior, though it doesn't explain the reasons behind this behavior.

### Secondary Research

This involves gathering market insights from information that others have collected directly from the customers. For instance, if you conducted primary research, and then shared it with the public, someone using this information for their research purposes would be conducting secondary research. Whereas primary research is useful for understanding your target customers, secondary research is quite useful for analyzing your competitors and the general market.

There are three main sources of secondary research:

- **Public sources:** These refer to information that is publicly available. You can find this information on online repositories, online portals for government statistics, such as the websites for the Bureau of Labor Statistics and the U.S. Census Bureau, industry magazines, and so on.

- **Commercial sources**: These mainly refer to market reports prepared by commercial research agencies such as Forrester, Pew, or Gallup. In most cases, you will need to pay for access to these reports.

- **Internal sources:** These refer to the data that you already have within your organization (for businesses that are already operational). These will include things like your customer acquisition costs, your customer lifetime value, your average revenue per sale, and so on. Basically, this is information you already have that can help you figure out what customers might want today.

When carrying out your market research, it is advisable to combine both primary and secondary research. Secondary research is great for getting a general feel of the market and learning about the trends within the market. However, everyone else also has access to much of this data, and therefore, if you stop here, you will probably glean the same highlights as everyone else. Conducting your own primary research will allow you to gather unique insights about the market and develop your own unique perspectives.

## STRATEGIES FOR MARKETING YOUR BUSINESS

Once you are done conducting your market research, the next step is to figure out the best strategies to market your business. Marketing is all about making the right customers aware of your products and services and making them connect with the value you are offering.

If you check online, you will find lots of 'gurus' claiming that this or that marketing strategy is the best. Some will say Facebook Ads are the best, others will say SEO is the best, and yet others will give that title to content marketing. However, here is the thing. No single marketing strategy can be termed as the best. The best marketing strategy depends on two things: what you are selling, and who you are selling to. That is why we started with market research, so that you would have a good understanding of who your customers are.

That said, there are some marketing strategies that have proven to be effective for a wide range of businesses. Before we look at these strategies, however, I want you to keep one thing in mind. You don't have to use them all in your business. Instead, what you want to do is to find those that work best for your business and your customers and focus on them. That's what matters.

Let's take a look at 10 popular and effective marketing strategies.

**Identity And Branding**

This is all about creating a company name and graphic elements –logo, imagery, brand colors, and so on– that communicate a very specific thing about your business. For instance, when you see the partly bitten-off Apple logo, you immediately think of great design and sleek, high quality tech gadgets. Simply looking at the yellow colored arched M that represents McDonald's immediately gets you thinking of their tasty burgers. Similarly, looking at the three pointed Mercedes-Benz logo brings about images of elegance and comfort.

You should start creating an identity and brand for your business right from the start. Start by thinking of a strategic name that communicates the qualities you want people to associate with your business, and then hire someone to come up with a nice logo and other brand visuals that embody these qualities. Even if you are on a tight budget, you can hire a freelance designer for a couple bucks. From there, make sure to use your visual identity in every place where a customer might interact with your business.

**Use Google My Business**

This is a Google powered service that allows business owners to promote their businesses to local markets. If your business is listed on GMB, it will appear among the top searches when people within that geographical area search for products or services that your business provides. The listing is accompanied by a profile of the business and reviews left by previous customers.

Appearing among the top results for searches related

to your products and services can drive a lot of traffic to your business. What's more, if you have great ratings, this will increase people's trust in your business. All this makes Google My Business a great option for marketing your business without spending lots of money. The best part is that you can easily increase your ranking on Google My Business by making sure you have an optimized profile and getting great reviews.

**Create A Professional Website**

Like I mentioned earlier, most customers will go online to research about a business or product before making a purchase decision. Therefore, you need to make sure that your business can be found online, and having a website is the best way to do so. Your business website acts as a digital business card and gives you the first opportunity to create a good impression of your business. Having a professional website allows potential customers to quickly know who you are, where you are located, what products and services you offer, and how potential clients can get in touch with you. Apart from making it easier for your business to be found, having a website creates customer trust and shows that you are a legitimate business.

A website also allows you to do several other things, such as sharing news about your company, showcasing customer testimonials, communicating your prices, collecting email addresses from potential clients, and so on.

Creating a professional website is very easy today, even if you do not have the technical expertise. You simply need to buy a domain name, buy hosting for your website, and then use a free CMS like WordPress to create your site. With a CMS like WordPress, there are several templates to choose from, so all you need to do is find one that works for you and replace the content with your own. However, if you feel that this is too difficult for you, you can always hire a web designer to build a website for your business.

**Content Marketing**

Content marketing is all about providing your customers with engaging, valuable content that helps your target market solve their problems and show your expertise in your industry. The content doesn't necessarily have to be promotional. For instance, if you are a car dealership, you could regularly create content that educates people about cars – how to

service their cars, how to improve their fuel effi-
ciency, safety tips, and so on. The point of content
marketing is to position yourself as an expert in your
industry, such that when a customer is ready to buy,
they will automatically think of you. Aside from
positioning you as an expert, content marketing will
also help drive lots of traffic to your business.

Content can take a wide variety of formats – articles
and blog posts, videos, audio, infographics, social
media posts, online courses, and so on. Similarly, the
content can be distributed through a wide range of
channels – social media, blogs, podcasts, YouTube,
and so on. You just need to determine the format
and channel that works best for your target
audience.

To be effective, you need to make sure that you are
producing high quality content on topics that are
relevant to your target audience. Your content
should also be SEO optimized to increase the
chances of people finding it organically. Done well,
content marketing is a great and inexpensive way of
marketing your business, building customer trust,
and growing your brand image. While the results
might take a while to materialize, the content will

continue driving traffic to your business long after you created it.

## Partner With Other Brands

As a new business, a lot of people do not know you yet. You can change this and quickly reach a wide audience by partnering with other brands within your industry that are not your direct competitors. For instance, if you just launched a car wash and detailing business, you could approach a car repair shop and offer free car detailing for their customers on your first month. Such an approach will allow you to tap into the other business' customer base and convert some of them into your customers as well.

## Use Social Media

No business can afford to ignore social media today. With over 2.65 billion people (more than one third of the world's population) on social media, it presents a perfect and inexpensive opportunity to get your business in front of its customers. Some businesses, actually operate purely on social media.

Using social media is as easy as creating professional social media profiles for your business, growing your following, and regularly posting your products, information about your company, and other relevant information. Social media also gives you a relatively cheap way of interacting directly with your customers.

Considering that every other business is on social media, you will need a social media strategy if you want your social media marketing efforts to be effective. Don't try to be active on every platform. This might end up being overwhelming for you. Instead, you should identify the platforms that your ideal customer spends the most time on and focus on these platforms. Second, determine the most effective forms of content, and then create a posting schedule. You will also need to monitor your results and regularly optimize your approach to ensure maximum results.

You can also make your social media efforts more effective by leveraging the power of influencers. Influencers are social media users with a large following and whose opinion on a certain topic is respected. Influencers can be very effective for things like growing awareness about your business or your products and services, growing your social media following, driving traffic when you have a sale or offer, or even launching your business. For best results, you should only partner with influencers who work within your niche. These influencers have demonstrated their expertise in the niche and have highly interested followers that are more likely to become your customers.

**Advertise In Print Media**

While online channels are increasingly taking over, traditional channels like print media are far from dead. Many newspapers and magazines still have a large number of readers, and advertising in such can help you reach a high number of people, especially those you would be unable to reach using digital marketing channels.

Advertising in newspapers is a great way of targeting people within a certain geographical area (such as a city, a state, or a country), while advertising in magazines is a great way of targeting people within a certain niche. For instance, if you are in the real estate business, you can reach your target market by advertising in real estate magazines. The fact that the popularity of print media is declining also means that advertising in print media is a lot cheaper today than it was a couple years ago.

That said, don't rely exclusively on print media

advertising. It should be used to complement your digital marketing efforts, since the majority of people today get their information from digital channels.

## Email Marketing

Email marketing is one of the most effective and most cost-efficient ways of marketing your business. With email marketing, you simply need to send periodic emails to your customers giving information about your products, announcing new products, giving information about sales and offers, and so on. Email marketing is easy to set up, allows you to reach thousands of customers with a single email, and the best part is that you can automate email marketing, allowing an email marketing campaign to execute automatically with no further input from you.

The only difficult part of email marketing is getting potential customers to give you their email addresses. However, there are several approaches you can use to collect client emails, including giving lead magnets, running contests and giveaways in exchange for email addresses.

## PPC Advertising

Pay-per-click (PPC) advertising is a digital marketing model that allows your ads to be shown whenever people search for products and services related to what you are selling. The great thing with PPC ads is that you don't pay for them to be displayed. Instead, you only pay for every time someone clicks on your ad. There are several platforms that offer PPC advertising, with the most popular being Google and Facebook.

For your PPC advertising campaign to be effective, you need to do proper keyword research and ensure that you bid on keywords that your potential customers are most likely to be searching for. Your ads are shown based on factors such as their relevance in relation to the keyword, the quality of the ad and your landing page, and so on.

**Posters, Flyers and Stickers**

If you are running a brick and mortar business and want to promote your business within a specific geographical location, posters and flyers can be quite effective. For instance, Reddit cofounder Alexis Ohanian attributes Reddit's early success to the $500 he spent on printing custom stickers for Reddit. He placed the stickers on street light posts, street signs, give them to passersby, shared them with fellow attendees at conferences, and so on. He says that this simple strategy helped Reddit gain a lot of users in its early days. Similarly, you can start promoting your business locally by putting up posters and handing out flyers and stickers to potential customers. It is a cheap and effective way of promoting your business.

**Referral Marketing**

This is a marketing approach where current customers and anyone else who knows about your business sends leads your way, typically in exchange for something, such as a discount, a freebie, and so on. Referral marketing can be very effective because it relies on word of mouth. According to a research by WOMMA, word of mouth marketing is five times more effective compared to other forms of paid advertising.

To use referral marketing, you need to determine what incentive you are going to offer in exchange for a referral, and then come up with a way of tracking referrals. Of course, for referral marketing to be effective, you need to make sure that you are offering high quality products and services. No one will want to refer their friends and family to you if your products and services are whack.

## SALES TECHNIQUES TO BOOST YOUR PROFITS

Like I mentioned, sales is the most important aspect of your business. If you are not making sales, your business is on its deathbed. Therefore, after using the techniques shared above to market your business, you also need to make sure that your customers are making the purchase. How do you do this?

Below are some techniques that will help you make more sales and boost your profits.

- **Focus on benefits:** A lot of entrepreneurs focus on the features of their products and services when selling. However, customers don't buy features. They buy results. Therefore, instead of talking about all the features of your products, talk about the benefits that the customer stands to gain by using your product or service.

- **Focus on the pain**: Customers are considering purchasing your product or service because they have a pain point that needs to be resolved. Instead of focusing on why they should purchase your product, focus on the pain they will continue to endure by not buying your product or service. Reminding them of the pain or cost of not solving the problem will convince them to buy.

- **Use testimonials**: Very often, customers are wary of buying a product because they are not sure whether it will give them the desired results. By showing testimonials from previous customers, you are moving from hypotheticals and showing the results that you have been able to achieve for others. You are getting rid of doubts by showing others who have tried and gotten satisfied with your products and services.

- **Preempt customer objections:** What are the main reasons customers refrain from purchasing from you? Are there objections that you have heard time and time again? Determine the top sales objections for your customers, and then instead of waiting for the customer to bring up the objection, preempt them and address these objections even before the customer brings them up.

- **Focus on helping:** Even though your main aim is to sell, you should focus on helping your customers. Therefore, don't just jump into the features and benefits of your products or try to sell a product the customer does not need. Instead, listen to the customer, find out their greatest problem, and focus on providing the best solution for their problem. This means that, in some cases, you might have to recommend a different product or service from what you are selling. However, the point is to create trust with your customers. Let them see you are on their side, and they will keep coming to you whenever they have a problem. Ultimately, selling your products and services is all about selling yourself. Customers are not only buying what you are offering, but they are also showing trust in you and what you are doing. If they don't trust you, you can rest assured that they are not going to buy from you, regardless of how good your products or services are.

Therefore, in addition to selling your products and services, you have to learn how to sell yourself. Below are some tips on how exactly to do that.

- **Tell your story:** As an entrepreneur, it will get to a point where the customer might want to understand what you are about. They will want to know why you are doing what you are doing. Therefore, you should create a compelling personal story to explain yourself and your business or company. What are your reasons for starting this business? What do you aim to achieve? What are your challenges? When you look at some of the biggest companies in the world, you will notice that they have such a story, and you need to create one for yourself as well. Having such a story will help customers build an emotional connection with your business, see the behind-the-scenes passion, and this will in turn, encourage customers to trust you.

- **Be Confident:** As an entrepreneur, you have to be confident in yourself and your products or services. Your customers are taking a risk by purchasing your products. If you seem unsure of yourself, they will take this as a sign that you do not believe in your products, and therefore, they won't believe in your products either. However, when you exude confidence, it shows that you know what you are talking about, which builds the customer's trust.

- **Build relationships:** Don't treat your customers as a means to an end. There are more to them than the profits they bring. Instead of focusing solely on making the sale, focus on building relationships with them. Pay attention to them as people, be friendly to them, listen to their needs, and focus on providing what is best for them. This is how you create loyal customers.

- **Show expertise:** The more of an expert you are, the more your customers are going to place their trust on you. Therefore, as an entrepreneur, you need to know your stuff. Have a good grasp of your market, your products, and your industry. Be willing to answer your customers' questions and offer them advice. Simply, take every moment as an opportunity to show how knowledgeable you are in your industry.

- **Remain professional**: Most importantly, you should always make sure that you come across as a professional. This means that you should always treat your customers well, be punctual with your appointments and meetings, dress well, have a professional email address, be reliable, maintain a positive attitude, be organized, be accountable, be respectful, and most importantly, be honest and trustworthy.

Below is a checklist to help you build a strong foundation for your customer acquisition process. For marketing and sales techniques, you can check the list off once your business is up and running.

**I have answered the following questions from my market research:**

☐ Who are my customers?
☐ What products are they using now?
☐ Why do they buy?
☐ Why would they buy from me?

**I have conducted the following types of primary market research:**

- ☐ Online surveys
- ☐ Telephone surveys
- ☐ Direct mail surveys
- ☐ Focus group surveys
- ☐ Face to face interviews
- ☐ Observation

**I have conducted secondary research from the following sources:**

- ☐ Public sources
- ☐ Commercial sources
- ☐ Internal sources

**I have/am going to use the following strategies to market my business:**

- ☐ Identity and branding
- ☐ Register my businesses on Google My Business
- ☐ Building a professional website
- ☐ Content marketing
- ☐ Partnering with other brands
- ☐ Social media
- ☐ Print media
- ☐ Email marketing
- ☐ PPC advertising

- ☐ Posters, flyers and stickers
- ☐ Referral marketing

**I am conversant with using the following sales techniques:**

- ☐ Focusing on benefits rather than features
- ☐ Focusing on customer's pain
- ☐ Using testimonials
- ☐ Preempting customer objections
- ☐ Focus on helping my customers

**I am using the following tips to sell myself:**

- ☐ Story telling
- ☐ Confidence
- ☐ Relationship building
- ☐ Showing my expertise
- ☐ Presenting myself as a professional

## SET UP YOUR TEAM

Most entrepreneurs start their businesses as a one man show. However, as your business grows, you will realize that it is impossible to take care of everything by yourself. If you want your business to continue growing, you will need to build a team to help you take care of various aspects of your business, such as sales and marketing, finance, operations, and so on.

The people you choose at this early stage of your business are very crucial to the success of your business. If you hire the wrong people when your business is still in the startup stage, they could easily run your business to the ground, no matter how good your products or services are. Therefore, resist the temptation to hire a friend or family member, and instead find people who are qualified for the position.

Here are some reasons why hiring the right people is very crucial for a startup.

- **Reputation**: As a new business, you are in the process of establishing your reputation. At this point, your first employees will be seen as the face of the business, and therefore, if you want your business to be known for qualities like professionalism and excellent service, you have to hire those who are the embodiment of these qualities.

- **Future**: The first few employees you hire when your business is still in its infancy will play a huge role in establishing a company culture for your business. Therefore, it is important to find right-minded, goal-oriented employees who will help create the right culture for your business.

- **Advocates:** If your first employees are passionate about your business and love what they are doing, they will act as advocates for your business, spreading the word about your business to their family and friends. This can help you acquire some of your first customers.

- **Funding:** Investors don't invest in ideas. They invest in people. Investors understand that it takes a great team to build a business from scratch and turn it into a profitable business. Therefore, investors will want to know if you have the right people before giving you their money. If you simply employed your siblings and friends despite their lack of expertise or experience, you will have a hard time convincing investors to give you their money.

- **Mistakes:** As a new company, you don't have room to make a lot of mistakes. Hiring the wrong person when your business is still in its early stages can cause damage that might take you years to undo. In some cases, you might not even recover from this damage. Therefore, you need to be very careful with your first hires, because these are the people that will help you turn your business from an idea into something great.

## HOW TO CHOOSE THE RIGHT EMPLOYEES

Having seen how crucial it is to hire the right employees, how do you go about choosing the right employees for your new business?

One mistake that a lot of entrepreneurs commonly make is to focus on their start-up status when hiring employees. However, here is the thing – your business won't be a start-up forever. Therefore, you need to think about the long term trajectory of your company even when hiring your first ever employee. You should try to hire employees who will possibly be the pioneers and leaders of their departments once your business starts growing. For instance, if you need help with marketing while in your startup stage, don't simply hire someone because they know their way around Facebook ads. Hire someone who has the potential to head your marketing department in the future. This way, once your business starts growing, there will be a leadership structure already in place, and it will be a lot easier for you to scale your business.

That said, here are some of the most important things to keep in mind when setting up a team for your new business:

## Go For Employees Who Know The Importance Of Customer Service

While customer service is important for every business, it is particularly important for a new business. At this time, you are trying to establish your reputation, and therefore, every customer interaction is an opportunity to build your reputation. In addition, since you don't have a large team, everyone will be involved in sales and marketing tasks. Therefore, you should focus on building team that places customers at the forefront.

## Find The Right Personalities

Working in a startup is very different from working in an established company. Startups are highly unpredictable. Things can change any minute. In addition, the leadership structure in startups is very different from leadership in established companies. Startups require risk taking and application of unconventional strategies.

Therefore, as much as you need to hire people for their talent and skills, you also need to make sure they have the right personality to fit in a startup. They should be able to think outside the box and come up with solutions. They should have the emotional fortitude to deal with the high stress that comes with working in a startup. You also want people who can take initiative when problems arise, even if the problems are not exactly within the definitions of their role. In other words, you want employees who have the entrepreneurial mindset.

## Put Attitude Into Consideration

When hiring for a startup, attitude is very important, even more important than skills. You can train and equip them with the proper skills, but it is way more challenging to change their attitudes. Like I mentioned earlier, working in a startup involves high levels of stress, and therefore, you want employees with a positive attitude. Employees who do not crumble at the first sign of pressure. People who believe that there is a solution to every problem. People who will maintain their composure even in the face of unreasonable customer demands. People who are open to learning and evolving.

## Aim For Diversity

Try as much as possible to avoid homogeneity when

building your team. If you hire people who have the same backgrounds, people with similar personalities, people who think the same, and people who work the same, you are setting yourself up for trouble. Such a team will have the same perspectives, and therefore there will be no room for creativity, which is critical for a new business. There will be a shortage of new ideas. Finally, you will never see trouble approaching, because everyone in your team has the same blind spots. To avoid this, try to make your team as diverse as possible.

## Go For Action Takers

I cannot stress this enough. The people you hire for your new business should be action-oriented. New businesses are fast paced. There's never time to sit around catching up on your friend's Facebook posts. There is a lot to do, and very often, the deadlines are tight. Therefore, you want people who will be able to hit the ground running. People who will see what needs to be done and take action without waiting for you to instruct them to do so.

## HOW TO GET YOUR NEW EMPLOYEES WORKING AS A TEAM

Once you have hired your new employees, you need to transform them from being solely employees, to being a team that works together like the parts of a well-oiled machine. If you want your new business to experience quick growth, you need to make sure that the team is greater than the sum of its parts. Question is, how do you transform employees from individuals into a team?

**Share Your Business Vision**

To make sure that everyone is on the same page, start by sharing your vision for the business. What are you trying to achieve? What are the goals of your business? What kind of business culture are you trying to build as your business grows? What kind of experience do you want customers to have when they interact with your business? The point here is to make sure that the goals of the business are clear to everyone, and that everyone is working towards the same goals.

**Understand And Utilize Each One's Strengths**

I already mentioned the importance of diversity

when hiring your employees. To make the most of this diversity, you need to understand each employee's individual strengths, and what they are bringing to the table. Utilize each employee's unique strengths and make it clear to them that what they do is crucial for the business. You want your employees to feel like they contribute. They need to feel like they have a strong purpose of being there, otherwise they may become disengaged and their productivity will tank. On the other hand, when everyone is utilizing their strengths and feeling that they play an essential part in the business, the overall team morale and productivity will be high.

**Get Everyone Involved**

Don't allow your employees to sit around idly. Get them engaged from the first day, let them hit the ground running. Involve them in the day to day running of the business, and encourage them to continuously learn and improve their skills. Challenge them to continuously push themselves and unlock their potential. Explain to them that their work is important for the growth of the company, and the more the company grows, the better the rewards they will get. Support and mentor them, and most importantly, recognize their effort and acknowledge their successes.

**Set Goals For The Team**

Aside from sharing your vision, get in the habit of setting goals together with your team, both long term and short term. Every task they undertake should be based on specific goals. Motivate them to hit these goals, and encourage them to work together. Working together towards specific goals and milestones will provide them with opportunities to help each other and gel together as a team. Constantly remind them that the success of the team is as important as individual success, and when they achieve their goals, recognize their efforts as a team.

## HOW TO KEEP YOUR TEAM RUNNING SMOOTHLY

Getting your employees to buy into your vision and work together as a team is not always enough. When you bring people together, it is for certain that there will be some friction here and there, and this is damaging to your business. So how do you minimize the friction and keep your business running smoothly.

## Define Roles Clearly

Make sure that each member of the team knows what their job is and what their responsibilities are. If roles are not clearly defined, not only will this cause tension between your employees, it will also affect productivity. For instance, let's assume that something needs to be done, but it is not clear whose responsibility it is. There is a chance that everyone will avoid doing it. Those who wait for the task to be completed so that they can do their part will be hindered to move forward as well. This means that no work will get done. In addition, the arguments over whose responsibility it is could lead to conflicts. To avoid this, make sure that everyone knows what their role is.

## Communicate

Communication is very important for the smooth running of a business, and it is up to you to create a culture of communication. Your employees are not mind readers. If you need them to do something, make it clear what you need them to do. If something was not done as you expected, let them know, make sure they understand how you expect things to be done. Don't be vague when communicating with your employees. Everything should be crystal clear.

This will eliminate confusion and ensure that things gets done properly.

In addition to communicating your expectations clearly, you should also provide channels for your employees to share their thoughts and opinions. Get in the habit of asking them for feedback, and make sure everyone has an opportunity to get their voice heard. When your employees know you value their opinions, they will be more invested in the success of your company. On the other hand, if they feel unheard and ignored, this will lead to resentment and frustration, which is bad for your team morale.

**Identify Problems Early**

Sometimes, there will be friction within your team. You might realize that someone is a natural trouble-maker after hiring them. Sometimes, employees will slack off due to personal issues. Some people might just not be a good fit for your business culture. If you don't want such people to poison your entire team, you need to identify such problems early and nip them in the bud. If someone is having personal issues, have a chat with them and discuss how they can resolve the problem without bringing their issues to work. If an employee is slacking, talk with them and come up with a plan on how they can improve their performance. In some cases, the best action to take is to fire that person. Do not waste resources, especially in the start-up phase, get rid off anyone that is not suited for business, just make sure to follow all labor laws when doing so.

## Show Your Employees That You Value Them

Don't just treat your employees as mere cogs that are only necessary for your machine to keep running. Show them that you care about them as people. Learn about their personal life, their families, and their hobbies. Be concerned about and support their personal growth. Help them achieve their career goals. Invest in them, and give them what they need to do their work well, including providing them with the right tools and creating a healthy working environment for them. Celebrate their victories, and overall, treat them with dignity.

## Build A Team Beyond Your Business

In addition to the team you have built inside your business, you can also build an external team. These are people outside your business that you have not hired directly, but who still make contributions to the successful running of your business. For instance, you can periodically invite guest speakers to talk to your internal team and help them improve their skills, invite key customers to meetings to get their feedback, have conversations with your key partners to improve collaborations, hire a coach to help your team increase productivity and so on. The point here is that you should not limit your team to your direct employees. Find ways for your outside contacts to contribute to your business.

CHAPTER FIVE CHECKLIST

Below is a checklist to help when you're in the
process of building a team for your business.

**I have looked for the following qualities when
hiring:**

☐ Employees who know the importance of
customer service
☐ Employees with the right personality
☐ Employees with the right attitude
☐ A diverse team
☐ Employees who are action-oriented

**I have done/I'm doing the following to get my
employees working as a team:**

- ☐ Shared my vision for the business
- ☐ Understood and utilized each employee's unique strengths
- ☐ Got everyone involved
- ☐ Set goals for the team

**I have done/I'm doing the following to keep my team running smoothly:**

- ☐ Defined roles clearly
- ☐ Communicated properly
- ☐ Try to identify problems early
- ☐ Show my employees that I value them
- ☐ Built a team outside my business

## LEGALIZE AND PROTECT YOUR BUSINESS

**B**efore you launch your new business, you will probably need to share your idea with someone else. For instance, if you don't have enough capital to kickstart your business, you will need to share your idea with financiers or investors before they can give you their money. So, how do you do this while at the same time making sure that they don't steal your idea and implement it themselves?

In addition, before opening up for business, you need to legalize your business to avoid any problems with the government. What steps do you need to take to ensure that your business is in compliance with all the legal aspects of running a business? In this chapter, we'll take a look at how to handle these things.

## HOW TO PROTECT YOUR BUSINESS IDEA

If you need some help bringing your business idea to life, there is always the risk that whoever you turn to for help – an investor, a bank, or a potential partner – might steal your idea and start the business without you. While you cannot completely eliminate this risk, there are some steps you could take to minimize the risk. These include:

**Don't Reveal Too Much**

If you need to borrow some money from someone in order to finance your business, or if you approach someone about partnering with you, they obviously need to know about your business idea. However, it is never a guarantee that the person will agree to give you their money or come on board as a partner. For instance, when the Winklevoss twins approached Mark Zuckerberg and asked for help building a social site, they shared the details of the site with him, but Zuckerberg denied their request and then went on to build a social site that was very similar to what they had described. If you don't want to end up in the same situation as the Winklevoss twins, you need to protect yourself by not revealing too much.

Question is, how do you convince someone to give you their money or partner with you while keeping the important information to yourself? The best approach here is to focus on the problem you are trying to solve and why you believe the idea will be profitable, without going into details about *how* you are actually going to solve the problem. If they show interest once they know the problem being solved and how profitable the idea could be, you can then have them sign a non-disclosure agreement (NDA) before you share the details of how your business will solve the problem.

However, it is good to keep in mind that many investors will be wary of signing NDAs. Investors receive lots of pitches, and signing an NDA might keep them from investing in other ideas that could be similar to yours. In this case, they might not be willing to sign a NDA, therefore, you might have to share your idea solely based on trust. Alternatively, you could consider the following approaches.

**Apply For A Patent**

If the success of your new venture relies on a new invention, then the best way to protect your idea is to apply for a patent for this invention. When you have a patent for the invention, others will be legally barred from reproducing your invention, using it, or making money from it for a specified period of time.

To patent your invention, you will need to apply for the patent from the US Patent and Trademark Office (USPTO). There are three types of patents. The first is the utility patent, which is the most common patent in the United States. This type of patent protects new and useful tools, machines, processes, matter composition, or article of manufacture. Utility patents protect your invention for up to 20 years.

The second type is the design patent, which protects inventions surrounding design aspects of a product. This type of patent prevents others from reproducing, using, or making money from products with the same design features as your patented design. A good example of a design patent is the unique shape of the Coca Cola bottle. Design patents will protect your design for up to 14 years. The third type and the least common is the plant patent, which is issued to people who invent or create new and distinct varieties of plants.

The problem with this approach, however, is that applying for a patent is very costly, and you might not have the money for that. In addition, patent applications take a while to get approved, and you cannot share the details of your invention before the approval, since the invention is not yet covered by the patent. To work around this, you can start by applying for a provisional patent. The provisional patent becomes applicable from the day of filing and protects your idea for 12 months from the day of filing. In addition, it is a lot cheaper than a non-provisional patent. Therefore, you can share your idea with potential investors or partners knowing that your invention is protected. However, you will need to apply for the non-provisional patent before the provisional patent expires, since the provisional patent is not renewable.

**Get Copyright Protection For Your Idea**

If your business is based on an original idea or a new work of art, rather than an invention, filing for a copyright certificate is the best way to protect your business. Whereas patents protect inventions, copyright certificates protect creative art. With a copyright certificate, you can protect artistic works, musical, dramatic, or literary works, scripts, architectural concepts, novels, poetry, songs, movies, and so on.

It's good to note, however, that the copyright certificate will not protect your idea. Instead, it protects your way of expressing this idea. For instance, if you have an idea for a novel, you cannot protect the idea. You have to come up with something tangible, such as a manuscript for the novel. Another person can create a novel based on the same idea, but they cannot reproduce your manuscript.

With copyright protection, you have the option of registering your creative work with the USPTO or not. Copyright protection applies automatically once you publish your creative work. However, it is advisable to register your work if you feel that you might have to sue someone for infringing on your copyright.

**Trademark Protection**

Whereas patents protect inventions, and copyright certificates creativity, trademarks protect brands. A trademark can be defined as a name, a phrase, a visual design, smell, or a sound that distinguishes your business or your products from those of competitors. Basically, anything that customers associate with your brand can be registered and protected as a trademark. Business/product names, logos, and slogans are the most common types of trademarks.

Just like with a copyright, it is not absolutely necessary to register your trademark with the USPTO. Simply using a name, slogan, logo, sound, or phrase in commerce gives you automatic claim to the trademark rights of that element. However, if someone infringes on your trademark rights and you decide to sue them, you will have to prove in a court of law that the trademark belongs to you, which can be a bit difficult. To avoid such problems, it is advisable to register your trademarks with the USPTO, since this will serve as evidence of your ownership of these trademarks.

Registering your trademark with USPTO also gives you protection across all states. Without registration, your automatic trademark protection only applies in the states where you have commercially used that mark. If someone else uses your trademark in a state where you have not used the mark commercially, you have no protection.

**Trade Secrets**

Trade secrets refer to information that has economic value, is not known by the public, and that which the owner has taken reasonable steps to ensure that it remains secret. Examples of trade secrets include processes, techniques, methods, devices, patterns, formulas, financial data, information about suppliers or customers, and so on. Therefore, if you have business processes or ideas that cannot be protected using patents, copyright certificates or trademark protection, you still have the option of protecting them as trade secrets.

Owing to their secret nature, you are not required to register your trade secrets with a federal body. Instead, if you decide to sue someone you believe has misappropriated your trade secret, it will be up to you to prove to the court that the information misappropriated meets the definition to a trade secret. Trade secrets are only protected in instances of misappropriation. In other words, the acquisition of this information must be accompanied by a nefarious act. For instance, if someone steals your trade secrets, or if an employee sells your trade secrets to a competitor, you have the right to sue. However, if you voluntarily share a trade secret without limitations, and the person uses this information to their advantage, you have no right to sue.

Trade secret protection remains in place until the information no longer has any economic value, the information becomes publicly known, or the owner stops taking reasonable measures to keep the information secret.

Trade secret protection is best used for ideas, processes, techniques, and inventions that can be used in secret and that are difficult to reverse engineer. For instance, the KFC recipe or Coca Cola formula are trade secrets because they are used in secret, and cannot be reverse engineered.

Sometimes, it might be necessary to use more than one of these methods to better protect your business idea. For instance, the Coca Cola bottle is covered by a design patent and at the same time it is covered by trademark protection, since consumers automatically associate the bottle design with the Coca Cola brand.

## HOW TO LEGALIZE YOUR BUSINESS

Your business is almost ready for launch, but there is one more thing you need to do – getting your legal ducks in a row. You don't want to find yourself facing numerous fines and penalties because you missed one small thing while setting up your business. Below are the steps you need to take to make sure that your new business is in compliance with all legal requirements.

**Conduct A Name Search**

You don't want to print out your business cards and put up a sign advertising your new business, only to discover that you are not legally permitted to use the business name you picked. Therefore, once you pick a name for your new business, you need to conduct a business name search to ensure that your chosen name is available for use and that the name does not infringe on the rights of another business.

Conducting a business name search is free, and can easily be done online. This is something you can easily do yourself without the need to hire an attorney. If you have plans of expanding your business beyond your state, make sure the name is available both within your state and in the rest of the country.

If the name is available, it is also advisable to conduct a trademark search to find out if anyone has trademarked the name. However, remember that trademark protection applies even when the owner hasn't formally registered the trademark, therefore do a thorough search to ensure that no one else is using the name commercially.

**Register Your Business**

Once you confirm that your chosen business name is available, go ahead and register your business. Registration gives your business the legal foundation to conduct transactions as an entity of its own. When registering your business, you will need to decide what business structure you are going to use. You can either register your business as a sole proprietorship or a partnership, a LLC, or as a corporation. The best business structure will depend on the nature of your business. We will take a look at the differences between these business structures and the advantages and disadvantages of each in the next section of this chapter.

**Get A Tax ID Number**

Once you register your business, it becomes a separate legal entity, and therefore, it will need to pay its own taxes, separate from your own personal taxes. For this purpose, you need to get Employer Identification Number (EIN) for your business. The EIN is also known as the Tax Identification Number (TIN). The EIN is like a personal social security number, but for your business. The EIN allows the IRS to track all transactions carried out by your business. You will also need the EIN in order to set up a bank account for your business. If you are setting up your business as a sole proprietorship, it is not absolutely necessary to get the EIN, but it is still advisable to get one, since it keeps your taxes separate from those of your business.

## Get The Required Business Licenses And Permits

Depending on the location where you will be primarily conducting your business, as well as the nature of your business and the industry you are involved in, you might need to get one or more business licenses from your county or city office, the state, or even from the federal level. For instance, if your business is in the food industry, you will need more licenses and permits than someone operating a computer repair shop. Some of the permits that you might need to obtain include the general business operation license, land use and zoning permits, permits from the health department, sales tax license, and so on. In addition, depending on the nature of your business, you might also need professional or occupational licenses.

## File For Trademark Protection

Like I mentioned in the previous section, filing for trademark protection is not absolutely necessary, since trademark protection starts applying immediately you use a name, logo, slogan, or other element commercially. However, registering your trademarks with the USPTO can make it a lot easier for you to claim this protection, especially in today's online environment where it is very easy for people to infringe on your trademarks. For instance, if someone registers a Twitter handle in the name of your business, you will have a hard time convincing Twitter that the name belongs to you if you do not have a registered trademark. However, if your trademark is registered, you will have the legal documentation required to show that the name belongs to you, and it will therefore be much easier for Twitter to transfer that handle to you.

## Set Up A Bank Account

Once you have registered your business and obtained a Tax Identification Number for the business, you need to set up a separate bank account for your business. Having a separate bank account for your business will make it easy to keep your personal transactions separate from your business transactions. This will be very useful when it comes to filing your business taxes. Depending on the nature of your business, this might be a mandatory step for you. All LLCs and Corporations are required to have a separate bank account from their owners.

## Get Acquainted With Employment Laws

Before you hire you very first employee, you need to make sure you are conversant with all employment laws. Seek the help of an employment law professional and ask them to ensure that you fully understand all your legal obligations as an employer. Some of the legal obligations you need to be conversant with include self-employment taxes, state and federal payroll and withholding taxes, employee wage and hour requirements, workers' compensation laws, unemployment insurance, OSHA regulations, anti-discrimination laws, and so on.

## HOW TO CHOOSE THE RIGHT LEGAL STRUCTURE FOR YOUR BUSINESS

We saw that before registering your business, you need to choose a legal structure for the business. This is a very crucial decision, since it will influence a lot of things, including your personal liability, the kind of paperwork you need to file, the day to day operations of the business, your ability to raise money, the amount you are going to pay in taxes, and so on.

Below are the different legal structures you can choose from.

## Sole Proprietorship

This is the simplest way of registering and operating your business. A sole proprietorship is also referred to as a DBA (Doing Business As). With a sole proprietorship, you represent your business and have complete control over the business. This means that the business does not exist as a separate legal entity, and therefore does not have its own separate assets and liabilities. The assets and liabilities of a sole proprietorship automatically transfer to the owner.

A sole proprietorship is a great choice if you are setting up a low-risk business, or if you want to test your idea at a small scale before expanding.

The downside with a sole proprietorship is that, since it is not a separate legal entity, you will be held personally responsible for liabilities of the business. For instance, if the business is unable to pay its creditors and meet other obligations, your personal assets might be used to cover these obligations. In addition, raising money as a sole proprietorship can be difficult, since banks are not too enthusiastic to finance sole proprietorships, and you cannot sell stock.

**Partnership**

This is another simple way of registering a business, but unlike a sole proprietorship, it involves a business that is owned by two or more people. Partnerships can be classified into two categories:

- **Limited Partnerships (LP):** These are characterized by one unlimited liability general partner, and one or more limited liability partners. The control over the company for the limited partners is also limited. The profits of the limited partnership are passed over to the owners, who then file their own personal tax returns. However, the unlimited liability partner will also need to file self-employment taxes.

- **Limited Liability Partnerships (LLP):** The difference between the LP and the LLP is that for the LLP, every owner has limited liability. In an LLP, no partner is held responsible for the obligations of the other partners.

If you want to register a simple business and also want to bring a co-founder or partner on board, a partnership is the way to go.

## Limited Liability Company (LLC)

This is a very popular business structure. An LLC is somewhat like a cross between a corporation and a partnership. Like a partnership, the LLC doesn't need the complex paperwork and formality of a corporation. At the same time, just like a corporation, an LLC acts as a separate legal entity, protecting you from taking over its liabilities. Therefore, if the LLC faces lawsuits or goes bankrupt, you don't have to worry about your personal assets being taken over to settle the obligations of the LLC. In most cases, the profits of the LLC are passed through to the owner, who then reports them under his or her own personal tax returns.

## Corporation

This is the go-to legal structure for large businesses that have a complex stock structure, those that want profits to remain within the company, or those that have plans to go public. Setting up a corporation involves a lot of paperwork and formality.

There are two common types of corporations:

- **C-Corp:** The C Corp is a separate legal entity that is legally liable for its own actions, makes its own profits, and pays income tax on its profits. C corps have the greatest degree of protection from personal liability for their owners. They are totally independent from their shareholders. C corps have the ability to raise money by selling stock. On the downside, C corps are a lot more costly to set up. They may also subject to double taxation – taxes are paid both on profits and dividends. C corps are great for medium and high risk businesses, as well as businesses that plan to go public or need to raise money.

- **S Corp**: These are similar to C corps, but are designed with the aim of avoiding double taxation. With S corps, profits (and sometimes losses) can be passed through to the owners, who then report them when filing their personal taxes. However, the tax obligations of the S corps vary by state. To set up an S corp, you need to register it with the IRS, in addition to registering it with the state. All the shareholders of an S corp need to be US citizens, and they should be less than 100 in number. This is a great choice for a C corp that wants to avoid double taxation.

# CHAPTER SIX CHECKLIST

Below is a checklist to guide you in the process of setting up your business.

**I have taken the following measures to protect my business:**

- ☐ Avoided revealing too much
- ☐ Applied for a patent
- ☐ Acquired copyright protection for my creative works
- ☐ Acquired trademark protection
- ☐ Taken steps to protect my trade secrets

**I have taken the following measures to legalize my business:**

- ☐ Conducted a business name search
- ☐ Registered my business
- ☐ Obtained a tax ID number
- ☐ Acquired necessary permits and licenses
- ☐ Filed for trademark protection
- ☐ Set up a bank account for my business
- ☐ Gotten acquainted with employment laws

**I have chosen the following legal structure for my business:**

- ☐ Sole Proprietorship
- ☐ Limited Partnership (LP)
- ☐ Limited Liability Partnership (LLP)
- ☐ Limited Liability Company (LLC)
- ☐ C corp
- ☐ S corp

# 7

# LAUNCH AND GROW YOUR BUSINESS

So far, you have taken all the crucial steps that you need to get your business off the ground. All that is remaining now is for you to launch your business, start making money, and grow and expand your business. However, this does not happen automatically. Don't think that all you need to do is open your doors for business and hope that customers will start streaming in.

If you want to achieve success quickly, you need to have in place measures that will bring attention to your business right from the first day, as well as measures that will keep your business growing. This is what we will cover in this chapter.

## PREPARING FOR THE LAUNCH

If you want a huge launch that will get customers streaming in immediately, you need to prepare for it beforehand. Preparation ensures that everything is in place and makes for a much smoother launch. Use the tips following tips to prepare for a successful launch.

### Do Some Testing

Creating a product and seeing it on the market can be quite thrilling. However, if you want your product to be successful, don't be in a rush to put it out into the market. Sure, you believe that your product is ready, and that it will perfectly solve the problem you are trying to solve, but what do your customers think? Before launching the product into the market, take a moment to test the product. Build a small group consisting of your target audience, share your product with them, and then allow them to share their views about their product.

The point here is that nothing beats the actual customer's perspective. You might think that your product is perfect, but the customers who will get to use the product might feel different. Testing your product on some customers before launch allows you to identify any possible flaws and make adjustments. This way, your product will be able to make the best possible impression at the time of launch. If you release a buggy product, customers might never give you a chance to redeem yourself.

## Get In Touch With Influencers

You want to bring as much attention as possible to your business and your products and services on launch day, and one of the best ways to do that is to work with influencers. As a new business, you obviously do not have a huge following online. Working with influencers allows you to tap into their audiences and spread word about your new business.

Don't wait until launch day to reach out to influencers. Instead, as part of your preparation, create a list of influencers within your industry and reach out to them in advance. Share your product with them, or invite them to experience your services. This way, by the day of launch, they will have interacted with your product and will be able to talk about it from a knowledgeable point of view.

## Develop A Schedule

Launching a new business can be a hectic affair, and if you are not careful, some things might get forgotten or overlooked, yet they could be damaging. To avoid this, you need to create a schedule. Decide the best time of the year for the launch –this is especially important for seasonal products– and come up with a list of the tasks that need to be completed before and during the launch, as well as the people responsible for these tasks. With such a schedule, you are more likely to hit your objectives.

## Identify Your Marketing Channels

How are you going to put word out about your new business? Are you going to use PPC advertising? Will you advertise in a popular magazine, or put up sponsored posts on popular blogs within your niche? Which social media channels are you going to use to promote yourself? Doing this early allows you to identify the marketing channels that are going to have the greatest impact.

## Get Your Team Excited

Finally, you need to get your team excited. Your employee's attitude and energy during the launch has an impact on potential customers' perception of your business and products. Therefore, in the days preceding launch day, make sure that your employers are well versed with your products and can easily and effectively answer customers' questions. They must know what is expected of them, and most importantly, be excited. Since they will be directly interacting with the customers, they will be laying the foundation for your brand reputation, which is why they need to be thoroughly prepared.

## SUCCESSFULLY LAUNCHING YOUR NEW BUSINESS

You have done all the preparation necessary, and finally, it's time to open your physical or virtual doors to the world. How do you bring maximum attention to your new business and attract as many customers as possible within the first few days?

Think of companies like Apple. They are able to sell millions of devices within a day or two of launching a new one. How do they do it, and more importantly, can you do the same? Maybe, maybe not. With the right approach, however, you might be able to do much better than expected. Below are some tips on how you should go about it.

### Build A Community

Don't wait to start finding customers for your business. Instead, start way ahead of the official launch day. Using channels like social media, start connecting with your audience, forging relationships with them and building a community. Share updates with them, interact with them, and get them ready.. This way, by the time you launch, you will have an excited community of people that will be waiting to buy your products. Their excitement will also build traction as these people share information about your business and products with their followers.

**Create A Pre-Launch Landing Page**

This point is somewhat related to the previous one. Don't wait until launch day to start finding customers for your products. Instead, start building up some hype about your products and set up a landing page to collect email addresses from those interested in your product. The landing page should have some information about your products, and it should get people to anticipate your launch. If possible, you can even include a timer to count down the time remaining before big day. This will get people curious and generate interest about your products. Finally, on opening day, you can send a blast email to everyone who shared their email address notifying them that you are now open for business.

## Host A Giveaway

The greatest way to get the business up and running is to get people excited about your products, and what better way to do this than by hosting a giveaway? After all, everyone likes the prospect of getting something for free.

With a giveaway, you will basically be giving potential customers a chance to win something in exchange for a specific action, such as following your business on social media, recommending your business to a friend of family, giving you their email address, or even buying a product.

The giveaway could be anything that gives value to a potential customer. This could be a physical product, a discount, a free service, a digital download, and so on. Of course, the giveaway should be related to your business. After all, the aim of the giveaway is to generate hype around it.

If you are launching your business online, you can easily host a giveaway using services like Rafflecopter, which allows you to set up contests and giveaways and share them via social media, blogs, websites, and so on.

## Call On Your Influencers

In the preparation stage, I already mentioned that you should identify and reach out to influencers within your niche and allow them to test your products and services. Now that they know what your products and services are all about, is the time for them to use their influence to bring attention to your business.

On launch day, have them put out content that will help drive traffic to your website or social media pages. They can do this through a variety of ways, such as posting reviews about your product or service, writing a story about your business, creating and pushing hashtags to create awareness, sharing visual content, sharing behind the scenes content, hosting contests, and so on. Basically, anything that will create awareness and get people interested in knowing more about your business.

**Create FOMO Around Your Products**

Depending on the nature of your business, you can offer a limited quantity of your products on launch day. The resulting fear of missing out (FOMO) will create more demand for your products and create a sense of urgency. In addition, once your first batch of products sell out, there will be greater hype as customers wait for the next batch, with a lot of customers hoping they will be lucky to snag your product this time round. This is why Apple fanatics queue overnight in front of Apple stores when a new iPhone is being released. They want to be among the first people to get their hands on the first batch of iPhones to hit the market.

For this tactic to be effective, you need to make it clear from the get go that there will be a limited quantity. If people don't know that the products are limited, they might assume that you planned poorly for the launch or that you do not have the capacity to meet demand.

**Turn Your Launch Into An Event**

Another great way of bringing maximum attention to your launch is to turn it into an event. Don't wake up one day, open the doors of your business premises and say that you have finally launched your business. Instead, you want your launch to be accompanied by the excitement of a big event. To use the example of Apple again, think about the release of a new iPhone. Apple holds an event and invites the media, tech bloggers, and other key stake-holders. In 2019, they even started livestreaming their launch event to the whole world.

Similarly, you can make your launch something big by turning it into an event. If you have the budget for it, hire out a venue, invite important stakeholders like potential clients, suppliers, and other high profile people, invite the media, hire a band or a comedian, and so on. Make your launch a big deal, and people will certainly treat it like a big deal. Something like this, however, usually works much better for already established businesses that are planning to release new products

## STRATEGIES FOR GROWING YOUR BUSINESS

Some entrepreneurs start a business and once it generates steady income, they then assume that all is done, that they can now sit back and start enjoying the fruits. However, if you are even mildly ambitious, this should not be enough for you. You should be on a constant lookout for growth opportunities. The more your business grows, the higher its chances of survival. Considering that the majority of new businesses fail within their first five years, then ensuring the growth of your yours is not a luxury. It is a matter of survival.

All companies started out small and grew into big,

thriving companies. With the right approach, you can guide your new business through a similar transition.

There are several strategies that a business can use to fuel growth. The strategy you choose will depend on your financial situation, the nature of your business, the nature of the competition you are up against, and even governmental policies.

Some of the most common business growth strategies are:

**Market Penetration Strategy**

This strategy involves finding ways to sell more of your existing products in your existing market. The market penetration strategy offers the least risk compared to the other growth strategies. Selling more of your existing products in your existing market is all about increasing your market share, which refers to the percentage of sales your business makes within a certain market compared to the total number of sales made by all competitors.

There are several techniques that you can use to increase your market share, such as lowering the prices of your products, increasing your promotion efforts, increasing your distribution channels, improving your products, getting non-buyers within your target market to start buying your products, and penetration pricing, where you start with low prices and then gradually increase them as you gain more market share.

## Market Expansion Or Development

This growth strategy involves finding ways to sell your existing products in a new market. Market development is a great strategy once you have maximized your market penetration, since it's more challenging to drive growth in your existing market by then. In such cases, the next logical step is to find a new market.

The easiest way market development tactic is to start offering your products and services in a different geographical location, such as a different city, a different state, or a different country. This is how some of the biggest businesses in the world today expanded their markets.

## Product Expansion Strategy

This growth strategy involves increasing your sales and profits by introducing new products to your existing product line and selling them to your existing market. This strategy is relatively low risk, since you already have the trust of your existing market. Think about Apple. No matter what product they release, they have consumers ready to purchase from the get-go.

One easy way of introducing new products to existing markets is to keep making improvements to your existing products. For instance, most smartphone companies keep releasing newer models of their smartphones every year. The people buying a new iPhone today are probably the same ones who are going to purchase the latest iPhone two years from now. Alternatively, you can create completely new products related to your current offerings.

## Diversification

Growing your business through diversification involves introducing new products to your product line and selling them to new markets. The new products could be related to your core offerings or totally unrelated. Since it involves selling unproven products in unproven markets, this strategy can be very risky, especially for small businesses. To use this growth strategy, you need to conduct lots of market research to determine whether the new market will be interested in your new products. This is almost similar to launching a new business. A good example of diversification is Google, an internet-oriented company, entering the autonomous car industry, or Apple, a computer manufacturer, introducing the first iPhone to make a foray into the smartphone market.

## Acquisition

This growth strategy involves a business expanding its sales and profits by purchasing another company and taking over its operations. Acquisitions are a great way for a business to add new products to its offerings and gain access to new markets.

There are three types of acquisitions;

- **Horizontal acquisition:** This involves buying business that are already competing against you, or businesses that operating in new markets that you want to enter (potential competitors).
- **Backward acquisition**: This involves acquiring businesses that are part of your supply chain, thereby giving you greater control over your production.
- **Forward acquisition:** This involves acquiring businesses that make up your distribution chain, thereby giving you

greater control over how your products are distributed.

Acquiring another business is a very costly affair, and therefore, before choosing this option, you need to be very clear on what you want to achieve out of the acquisition. However, despite the huge investment requirements, acquisition is not as risky as diversification, because the business you are going to buy is already established and has proven itself to the market. Still, you should opt for acquisitions as a way of growing your business after you have exhausted all the other growth strategies discussed above.

When it comes to growing your business with the above strategies, it is advisable to focus on one strategy at a time and exhaust it fully before moving on to the next. Focusing on several growth strategies at the same time can backfire terribly for your business.

Below is a checklist to help you prepare for your business launch and to grow your business thereafter.

**I have done the following in preparation for my business launch:**

- ☐ Conducted proper testing
- ☐ Reached out to influencers
- ☐ Created a schedule
- ☐ Identified my marketing channels
- ☐ Gotten my team excited for the launch

**I am going to use the following strategies to ensure a successful launch:**

- ☐ Build a community before launch
- ☐ Create a pre-launch landing page
- ☐ Host a giveaway
- ☐ Enlist the help of influencers
- ☐ Create FOMO around my products
- ☐ Turn my business launch into an event

**I have used the following strategies to grow my business (tick these off once your business is already operational)**

- ☐ Market penetration
- ☐ Market development
- ☐ Product expansion
- ☐ Diversification
- ☐ Acquisition

# 8

## GETTING IT DONE IN 30 DAYS

So far, I have shared with you all the information you need to start your own business, from conceptualizing your business idea and validating it to launching the business and planning for its growth.

At the start of this book, however, I not only promised to teach you everything you need to know about starting your own business, I also promised that I would show you how to get it all done within 30 days.

In this chapter, I am going to give you a breakdown of how you need to schedule all the activities described in this book to ensure that your business is up and running within 30 days. This is the most exciting part, because you are now getting into the doing part. As you go about getting these tasks done, you can keep referring to the relevant sections within the book to help you complete the tasks successfully.

Before we get started, I would like to mention that while it's possible to get everything done in 30 days, it is not a must. If you're someone who has absolutely no business experience, I would suggest to view the action-plan as steps to take within a certain period. That period, however, doesn't have to be 30 days. It could be 45, 60 and even 90 days. What's most important is that you plan it out in advance and refer back to the plan whenever necessary.

Let's get started!

**Day 1: Brainstorm Business Ideas**

A business idea is the seed that gives birth to a business, and therefore, the very first day should be spent brainstorming various business ideas. Think of as many business ideas as possible and write them down in a notebook. You can always refer to chapter one to help you come up with ideas. By the end of day 1, you should have a list of about 5 – 10 business ideas.

### Day 2 – 3: Evaluate Your Business Ideas

Go through the business ideas you came up with and try to determine whether they are viable by asking yourself the three questions we covered in chapter one: Is there competition in the space you want to enter? Is the competition making money? Can you come up with a better product or service?

This will require you to do some research, which is why you have two days to work on this task. By the end of day 3, you should have discarded some of your ideas to remain with a shortlist of business ideas that are viable.

### Day 4: Pick The Most Viable Idea

From your shortlist, pick one idea that you believe is the most viable – the one that has the highest potential for success. By the end of day 4, it should be clear to you which business you are going to start.

### Day 5: Determine The Ownership Of The Business

Are you going to start the business alone, or do you need partners? If you need a partner, have a conversation with them and determine how the business will be owned. Are you going to own the business equally? How much money will each of you invest? What will be each partner's role in the business? Deciding on these issues early on will prevent problems down the road.

## Day 6: Create An Initial Ownership Agreement

Having discussed the ownership of the business with your partners, draft an initial ownership agreement describing all the partnership terms you outlined yesterday and have all the partners sign it.

## Day 7: Pick A Name For The New Business

Depending on the ownership of your business, you can either do this alone or with a partner if you have one. Brainstorm on possible business names that give customers a good idea of what business you will be doing and present the kind of image you want your business to be known for. Try to come up with simple but unique names that will be easy for customers to identify. After brainstorming several names, pick one that best represents your business. Once you settle on a name, perform a business name search to make sure that nobody else is doing business under this name. I also recommend doing a domain search to make sure the domain related to your business is available.

At the end of day 7, you should be clear on what name you are going to use for business.

## Day 8: Choose Your Business Slogan And Design A Logo

Having decided on a business name, the next thing is a great slogan to use alongside it. You want a simple phrase that represents what you want your business to be known for, and one that customers can easily remember and associate with your business. Come up with several slogans and pick one that best represents your business.

Once you have picked a slogan, it's now time to design a great logo that will be used as a visual identifier of your future business, an image that will make people think of your business every time they see it. If you are not a good designer, you can hire someone to design the logo for you.

At the end of day 8, you should have a slogan and a logo for your business (or a designer working on your logo).

## Day 9: Conduct Market Research And Identify Your USP

Conduct market research to create an in-depth definition of your target market, and the reasons why this market will buy your products or services. You will also identify how big the market is, the different segments within the market, and the trends within the market, as well as the competition you are going to be dealing with.

Your findings should also help you to come up with a unique selling proposition that is going to help you differentiate your products and services from those that already exist in the market.

**Day 10: Create A Sales Forecast**

Using the data collected during your market research yesterday, come up with a sales forecast to predict the sales figures you expect your business to hit once you launch.

**Day 11: Estimate Your Startup Costs And Create An Expense Budget**

Start by noting down all the one-time expenses that you will have to cater for in order to get your business running. These include things like lease costs for your premises, costs associated with acquiring equipment, legal fees for registering your business, cost of acquiring inventory, website set up costs, costs associated with hiring employees, and so on.

Include everything that you need to pay for before you can start doing business.

From there, create another list of expenses for the recurring monthly costs. These include rent, payroll, utility costs, marketing costs, supplies, business insurance, and so on.

By the end of day 11, you should have a clear idea of the amount of money you need to start your business, and the amount of money you need each month to keep the business running.

## Day 12: Create A Marketing Plan

Armed with your market research, your USP, and your sales forecasts (sales targets), come up with a marketing plan that is going to help you attract the right customers in enough numbers to allow you to hit your sales targets.

## Day 13 – 14: Create A Business Plan

Spend these two days developing your business plan. You have already worked on some parts of your business plan, such as the market research, the financial projections, the marketing plan, and so on. Add these to your business plan and work on the missing parts. Creating the business plan requires some effort, which is why we are setting aside two days for this activity.

## Day 15: Identify Your Sources Of Funding

At this point, you have a clear idea of the amount of money you need to get your business going. It's now time to start thinking about where this money is going to come from. Are you going to use your savings? Will you borrow the money from friends and family? Will you approach investors and financiers?

If you are going to borrow money from your family and friends, start the conversations with them. If you are going to approach financiers and investors, find out what funding options they have and what you need to be considered for the funding. If there are any forms to be filled, collect them today.

## Day 16: Build A Website For Your Business

Don't wait until your business is up and running before you start thinking of building a website. The earlier you create an online presence for your business, the better. Decide what kind of website you want for your business and start building it. Like I mentioned in chapter four, you can build a website yourself using templates, even if you have no technical skills. If you find it difficult to do yourself, however, you can go ahead and hire a web designer to do it for you.

## Day 17: Create Your Social Media Profiles

When conducting your market research, you identified the social platforms where your target market spend most of their time. Today, spend the day creating and customizing social profiles for your business on these platforms and getting your first few followers.

## Day 18: Find Premises For Your Business

Decide the characteristics that define the most ideal business location, based on the nature of your business, and spend the day finding such a location. You will need the whole day to explore different locations and find one that is best suited for your business. Alternatively, depending on what type of business you're planning to launch, you can build a home office and upgrade later on.

## Day 19: Lease The Premises

Once you have found a location that is ideal for your business, spend this day getting in touch with the owner of the premises in order to get and sign a lease agreement. Try to go for a long term deal, as it is cheaper in the long run. If you choose a home office instead, spend the day setting it up.

**Day 20: Start Building A Team**

Your business plan includes the different people you will need to ensure the proper running of your business. Start identifying the people who can fill these roles, get in touch with them, and hopefully sign employment agreements with them.

**Day 21: Legalize Your Business**

You need to have your legal ducks in a row before you can open up for business. Spend this day registering your business, applying for a tax ID number, and obtaining the necessary permits and licenses. You can refer to chapter six as you go through this step. You can also use this day to find a great local business attorney. This is someone whose advice you will need from time to time over the course of running your business.

**Day 22: Set Up A Business Bank Account And Your Accounting Software**

Decide on the bank where you are going to have your bank account and set up the account. It is advisable to shop for a bank that will be willing to advance you credit in case you need money to grow your business.

Setting up your business bank account is unlikely to take you much time, therefore you can also spend the day shopping for and setting up your accounting software. Getting an accounting solution before your business is up and running will ensure that you have a proper record of all transactions from day one..

**Day 23: Apply For Funding**

You spent day 15 identifying possible sources of funding, determining the requirements, and collecting any forms you might need to fill. Now fill the forms as required and spend day 23 making the applications. It is important to apply at this time to ensure that you will have already received feedback by the time you are ready to launch.

**Day 24: Make Promotional Material And Start Spreading Word About Your Business**

Spend the day having promotional material like business cards, brochures, and flyers printed. For these, you will probably need to hire someone to design and print them for you. Ensure your promotional material looks impressive and contain all the necessary information about your upcoming business.

You should also start talking to people–your family, friends, and acquaintances –and letting them know that your business is launching soon, as well as explaining what your business will be offering and its benefits.

**Day 25: Purchase Inventory**

If your business is involved in the selling of goods made by another company, spend the day acquiring your inventory. If you need any special tools to run your business, acquire them today so everything will be already set up ahead of the launch day.

**Day 26: Plan Your Opening Event**

Create a plan for your opening day and make sure that everything is in place for a big and successful launch. You can also reach out to potential influencers and enlist their help in promoting your business on opening day.

**Day 27: Start Building Hype About Your Launch**

Don't wait until D-day to announce your business. Using your social media pages, and with the help of influencers, start creating some buzz about your upcoming launch. You want to get as many people as possible looking forward to your launch event.

## Day 28: Create And Send Out Invitations For Your Launch Event

Now that people are anticipating your upcoming launch, spend the day creating invitations for your launch event and sending them out to the people you want to grace it. These could be your suppliers and other business partners, influential people within the society, the media, and potential customers.

## Day 29: Make Sure Everything Is Ready For Launch

With the D-day just a day away, spend this day ensuring that everything is ready for launch. Make sure your team is ready and everyone knows what is expected of them, that the products are ready, that the venue is all set, and so on. You don't want any unwanted surprises on launch day.

## Day 30: Launch And Start Selling

Finally, hold your launch event, open your doors for business and start selling!

By following the above schedule, your business will be up and running within 30 days. Of course, as I mentioned earlier, the schedule is only meant to act as a guide. If you feel that you need more (or less) time on a certain task, feel free to adjust it.

I will say this again. What is most important is that you take action and actually get started. Customize the plan if necessary and get going!

It's very normal for beginners to get lost in the process. Some will get stuck and others will focus on unrelated tasks. This is where the guide will help you to get back on track and direct you in right direction.

FINAL WORDS

This book has covered a lot of information about how to start a business, and I hope that by now, you are confident in your ability to start your own business from scratch and build it into a successful business.

**Below is recap of everything we have covered in this book:**

In chapter one, we covered how to cultivate the entrepreneur mindset. We also covered how to come up with profitable business ideas and how to validate them.

In chapter two, we covered what a business plan is, why you need one, and how to write a business plan, going into details about all the elements that you need to include in your business plan. I also provided you with a template that you can use to develop your own business plan.

In chapter three, we covered the different ways of raising funds for your new business, how to keep good financial records and keep your business organized and why you need to keep proper records, as well as how to track your expenses and profits.

In chapter four, we covered all the aspects of selling yourself to customers, including how to know more about your customers by conducting market research, how to market your business, and various sales techniques you can use to increase your profits.

In chapter five, we covered the reasons why you need to hire the right people, how to choose the right employees, how to get your employees working as a team, and how to keep your team running smoothly.

In chapter six, we went over how to protect your business idea when reaching out to potential partners, investors and financiers, how to legalize your business, and the different kinds of legal business structures.

In chapter seven, we went over how to prepare for

your business launch, the different techniques you can use to ensure a successful business launch, and the various strategies you can use to grow your business after launch.

Finally, I provided you with a timeline to guide you on what you need to do every day to make sure that your business is ready for launch within 30 days.

Now all you need to do is to implement the information and strategies you have learned in this book, follow the guide, and you will be ready to launch your business in 30 days, just as I promised you would when you started this book.

Remember, like billionaire Richard Branson once said, business ideas are like buses. There is always another one coming. What matters is the execution of the idea. Therefore, stop sitting and dreaming about starting your business and quitting your job. Instead, implement what you have learned and get started!

Finally, if you enjoyed reading this book, I would appreciate it if you left a review. Thank you, and good luck as you embark on your entrepreneurial journey.

Printed in Great Britain
by Amazon

16403401R00113